™

Uncovering the Truth
You <u>Know</u> You Know

Karyn Henley

Karyn Henley Resources

Learn more at **www.LoveTrumpsKarma.com**

Love Trumps Karma: Uncover the Truth You <u>Know</u> You Know
by Karyn Henley

Copyright ©2005 Karyn Henley. All rights reserved. Exclusively administered by Child Sensitive Communication, LLC.

Cover Layout: Larimore Henley
Cover Illustration: Copyright © 2005 Raygan T. Henley. All rights reserved. Used by permission.
Cover Background Photo: comstock.com. Used by permission.

All poetry by Karyn Henley unless otherwise noted: © 2005 Karyn Henley. All rights reserved.

The dandelion logo is a registered trademark of Karyn Henley.

For permission to copy excerpts from this book, contact Karyn Henley, POB 40269, Nashville, TN 37204. office@karynhenley.com

ISBN 0-9743197-8-3

Contents

A down-loadable leader's study guide is available online for those who want to use this book as a 13-week course of study. You can find it at

www.lovetrumpskarma.com.

Acknowledgements

Each of us is a collection of thoughts, feelings, and ideas that we've gathered from all the points our lives touch. I'm no exception. There are hundreds of people who have influenced me through books or classes or discussions over dinner, not the least of whom are my parents, my sisters and their husbands, my own husband Ralph, my sons Raygan and Heath, and my daughter-in-law Mary Ellen. Many thanks to all of you. I owe thanks even to people with whom I've disagreed over the years, because they challenged my thinking. Whether I agreed with all of you or not, you've all sent me searching for more of God. Who could not be thankful for that?

I have special thanks to give to Mary Ellen Henley, Caryl Parker, Larimore Henley, Kristi West, Barbara Collins, Deonne Beron, and Gary Pigg. Each of them waded through the early drafts of this book in manuscript form, and they let me know whether they could sink or swim in it. I'm thankful none of them drowned.

I am most indebted to Ken and Sandra Rideout. Ken was a missionary in Asia, mostly Thailand, for 44 years. During those years, he allowed God to teach him many of the concepts around which this book is structured. I volunteered to help him organize his notes for a book he wanted to write with Sandra, and in so doing, I found my own heart challenged, enriched, and enlightened. Working with Ken and Sandra was truly a gift from God. It is with Ken's permission that I incorporate many of the thoughts that you will read here. He even allowed me to lift passages from his book and weave them into mine. Many thanks, Ken and Sandra.

Of course, my greatest thanks go to the One Who Was and Is and Is to Come. In the ocean of eternity, I'm simply a speck. But He sees me, and somehow this speck matters to Him. For that, He has my undying gratitude.

Chapter 1

Is God Playing a Trick?

Starbucks
New York City
Summer, 2003

Adam wove his way to the only vacant table, settled in, and tasted his chai. Full. Spicy. Maybe his life would be that way now. He had been in New York for only six weeks. Classes at the university were starting to feel routine, and he already had several new friends. One of them, Mei Li, plopped down in the cushy chair across from him. "What did you get?" asked Adam.

"Frappucino," said Mei Li. "Mocha." She closed her eyes and sipped.

Adam studied the ink-black brush strokes on Mei Li's tee-shirt. "What does the writing on your shirt say?" he asked.

Mei Li opened her eyes and looked down. "This? These are the Chinese characters for *Peace*." She pointed to Adam. "What's on yours?"

Adam had to look. He was relieved when he saw it wasn't a mustard stain. "It's a cross."

"Does it stand for anything?"

"Well, yeah," said Adam. "It means I believe in Jesus."

Mei Li rested her elbows on the table. "What does *that* mean?"

Adam took a swig of chai. What *did* believing in Jesus mean? Obeying the Ten Commandments. Going to church. Reading the Bible. Listening to Christian music. It suddenly sounded kind of shallow. And. . . well . . . now that he thought about it, he wasn't sure he really believed all that himself. But then, what *did* believing in Jesus mean? He took another swallow of chai, looked at Mei Li and shrugged. "I don't know," he said.

Nashville, Tennessee
Fall, 2004

"There's Pepsi and diet Pepsi in the fridge," said Emily. "Popcorn's coming." She shoved the flat bag of kernels into the microwave, snapped the door shut, and punched the snack button. The microwave hummed. She turned around and watched her friends opening chips and dips and drinks. They seemed to be making the new girl Tara feel welcome. Emily felt sorry for Tara having to move here just before her senior year. Emily would have hated leaving all her friends to move to a place where she didn't know anyone.

Emily's friend Kate grabbed a handful of chips. "As soon as the popcorn's done, let's go sit on the side porch," she said.

Tara skimmed one chip across the onion dip. "I love the way the side porch overlooks your yard, Emily. The birdbath. The garden. In the moonlight it's so Zen."

"Zen?" said Kate, a chip halfway to her mouth.

"Very peaceful," said Tara. "Very Zen."

"Isn't Zen a religion of demon worship?" asked Phoebe, clinking ice into her glass.

Tara's eyebrows went up, and she laughed. "Of course not," she said. "It's just a very peaceful religion. What religion are you?"

"Well. . .all of us are Christians," said Phoebe.

"That's nice," said Tara. "Whatever works for you. All religions are good. You know, whatever brings you to the spiritual Energy."

Phoebe's mouth was open, but Emily could tell that Phoebe couldn't find any words.

The microwave beeped, and Emily pulled out the hot bag. A buttery aroma filled the air. "Popcorn anyone?" she called.

Burlington, Vermont
Spring, 2002

Daniel's English class scooted their chairs into a circle, the way they did every Friday. Everyone flipped through their notebooks and pulled out the poems they'd been assigned to write. One by one, each person read his or her poem aloud.

Zoe's poem was about an angel appearing to a girl named Mary who was smoking in the girl's restroom. The angel told Mary she would have a baby. Everybody laughed.

Daniel was shocked at first, thinking the poem was irreverent. On the other hand, it made Daniel wonder what if. What if Gabriel really had appeared to Mary that way, in today's world?

After Zoe's reading, students began discussing the poem. "Daniel, do you have any comments?" asked Mr. Tolan.

Daniel scratched his ear. "Well. . .I think the angel and Mary are very powerful archetypes. They hold a lot of strong meaning. I wonder if you've thought about all the symbolism that people might read into the poem. I mean, does the baby grow up to save the world or die for someone or anything like that?"

Zoe wrinkled her nose. "I'm not very religious," she said. "I only recently found out that Christmas and Easter had something in common."

"Good point about the symbolism, Daniel," said Mr. Tolan. "Anyone else notice that?"

The discussion went on. Daniel wondered who else had no idea what Christmas and Easter were really about.

Northridge, California
Fall, 2001

Meggie joined the rest of her geology class around the sand table at the front of the room.

Mr. Rhinehart had tilted the table and was now pouring water onto the rocks and sand in it. "Millions of year ago, as the Ice Age came to a close, the glacial melt raised the ocean levels and sent rivers streaming overland, carving out canyons like so."

The water trickled over the sand and began washing out a path the length of the table.

"Of course *some* people say a great big finger came down out of the sky and formed canyons like this, Meggie." Mr. Rhinehart glared at her as he drew his finger through the sand, making a small gorge.

Atlanta, Georgia
Winter, 2004

Derek sprawled across the couch, reading his lit assignment. His little sister Berry pranced through the room and into the kitchen, where Mom was stirrng up some dinner.

"You know, I think there are lots of gods," said Berry. "Jesus is just one of them."

Derek shot his gaze through the kitchen door. This was going to be good.

Mom's eyes were wide, her mouth had dropped open, and her spoon was frozen in time, dripping over the bowl. "What makes you say that?" Mom said at last.

"My teacher told us that at school," said Berry. "And I think she's right."

> *From* True Believer *by Virginia Euwer Wolff:*
> *"I don't mean to be mean to Jesus in my thoughts. . . But I don't get how he hates so many millions of people and sends them down to Hell."*

Thailand
University of Chulalongkhorn

Ken Rideout lived in Thailand as a missionary for over 40 years. As well as going to Thai villages to teach and preach, he also taught classes in schools and universities. During one of his classes, several young men were laughing and talking, so Ken asked them what they were talking about.

One of the young men stood. "You foreigners travel 12,000 miles to tell us God loves us, God is love, Jesus is God's Son," he said. "You expect us to believe that Jesus raised the dead, walked on water, and did other miracles. Yet you tell us that if we do not believe your Jesus, we will die and perish forever, condemned by your God. Yours is just a narrow-minded religion. Our religion is broad. We do not condemn anyone. When we listen to you Christians, we see that some of you do not even believe that the other Christians are being saved. You condemn one another. We don't even know which missionary teaches the truth."

Another student asked, "Why do you believe that Jesus is God's Son?"

"The Bible teaches that He is," Ken answered.

"Why do you believe the Bible?" the student asked.

A third young man said, "You say God created the heavens and the earth and the first man and woman. God put the man and woman in the Garden of Eden, a paradise where there was no death and no sin. Then this Satan came and tempted them. Who created Satan? Where did he come from? Did God create Satan to tempt people? Then you say that because of this sin, death came upon the world, and the man and woman were cast out of the Garden of Eden. Wickedness and corruption came into the world. Then God sent Jesus to die for the sins of the people. All who believe on Jesus can be saved and go to heaven. All who do not believe will die condemned. You say heaven is a paradise. Will there be sin there, as there was in the paradise of Eden?"

"There will be no sin in heaven," Ken said. "For Satan and his angels will be destroyed."

"Why didn't God do that the first time, instead of leaving sin and wickedness, pain and torture in the world?" the student asked. "You say that the masses of the world are going to perish under God's condemnation. What is God doing? Playing a game?"

* * * * *

Asking Questions

All of these scenes are based on true stories. Except for the last scene, names and places have been changed so no one gets embarrassed that their story is being told. I've chosen these stories, because they represent the real world we live in. You probably have experienced similar situations yourself. If you haven't, it's almost a sure thing that within the next few years, you will.

You've also probably been taught a lot about the Bible, about Jesus, about the way Christians should talk, act, and worship. And somewhere along the way, you've probably become a believer yourself. Why? Why do you believe?

Do you have Buddhist friends yet? If you don't, you probably will. All of their lives, your Buddhist friends have been taught, "Do good. Do good. Do good." They have been taught the Buddhists' five precepts:

1. I will refrain from destroying life.
2. I will refrain from taking what is not given.
3. I will refrain from wrong-doing in sexual desires.
4. I will refrain from false speech, that is lies, backbiting, harsh speech, and idle chatting.
5. I will refrain from distilled and fermented intoxicants which produce heedlessness.

On the other hand, you were taught to follow Jesus' teachings and the Ten Commandments, which include "Do not murder. Do not steal. Do not commit adultery. Do not lie." These commandments sound a lot like the Buddhist's five precepts.

You may also have (or you will have) friends who are Jewish, Muslim, or Hindu. Most of them will be good people, good neighbors who give and serve and help. Many of them will be kinder and less judgmental of you than some Christian people you know. Are Christians any better than they are? What makes *your* beliefs right?

> ... we are going to take a look at what we all, as human beings together on this planet, have in common.

Lots of Christians are afraid to ask these questions. Some of them are afraid to even think about *karma* or *dhamma* (also known as dharma) or the *Supreme Brahman* or the *Tao* or *Zen*, probably because they think these religions are just demon worship. And while some of these religions do believe in demons (though they try to appease them rather than worship them), that is not all that these religions teach, and it does not hurt to learn about these religions. Some people don't want you to look into these religions, because they are afraid you will be deceived and convert to Zen or Taoism or something.

But it's important to figure out what you believe and why. So, while we're *not* going to do an in-depth study of Buddhism, Hinduism, Judaism, Taoism, and Islam in this book, we *are* going to take a look at what we all, as human beings together on this planet, have in common. We are going to look for the truth that we *know* we know. And after you've gone through this book, more than likely you'll never again have to wonder what you believe or why.

Two Dimensions

Listen to the news. Read a magazine. Watch television talk shows. Everyone wants to know the *real* stories of people's lives. We want to know the *truth* about who's innocent and who's guilty in the business scandal or the government cover-up or the shocking crime. And what about the health reports? Carbs are bad for you. No, meat is bad for you. No, meat is good for you. Fats are bad for you. No, fats are good for you. Chemical additives are bad for you. Natural remedies work wonders. Natural remedies are too weak to be effective. People study these things all the time, searching for the truth. Scientists, paleontologists, astronomers, chemists, all want truth.

When people believe something is true, they take a stand for it. If they believe it strongly enough, they might die for it. So it's important to know what you believe and why you believe it. And if you're going to go to all the work of building your life on your beliefs, depending on your beliefs to guide your choices about how to speak and act and handle failure and success, you might as well do your best to make sure that what you believe is true.

In that case, the first question is probably, "What is truth anyway?

Some people say, "There is no absolute truth." Hmmm. Is that statement an absolute truth?

truth and Truth

"This is a table," you might say. You knock on it with your fist and find that it's hard. That's true. You notice that the table is brown. That's also true. These descriptions are facts that are true at the moment. But the table may not always be brown. Someone might paint it a different color. It might fade in the sun, or get scratched or broken. And someday it will be tossed out. The kinds of truths that we touch, smell, and taste are truths that are only temporary, not permanent. They are *truths* in the physical dimension, not *Truth* in the spiritual dimension.

This kind of thinking is not new. As long ago as 540-475 B.C., the Greek philosopher Heraclites taught that the world was always changing, so it wasn't permanent. He said you can't put your foot in the same river twice, because the water you stepped into has gone by the time you take your foot out. By the same logic, it's not the same foot, because some of the cells have died and fallen off, and your foot is older, if only by moments.

Gautama Buddha, who lived in India from 563-483 B.C., also taught that everything was constantly changing. He said that the world around us is only an illusion, a physical realm in which nothing stays the same. Today, we know that this is scientifically correct. A table may look solid, but it's really made of atoms and molecules banging around. So in reality, the table is constantly changing.

Spiritual Truth is the only truth that doesn't change. Spiritual Truth is Knowledge and Wisdom that doesn't pass away. We can find this permanent Truth only in the spiritual world, the eternal dimension. (To keep it straight that we're talking about spiritual Truth, from now on Truth in the eternal dimension will start with a capital T.) So we actually live in two dimensions. One dimension contains the truth of this world, a body of information, a collection of facts that are temporary. The other dimension is the spiritual, the realm of permanent Truth.

GOD	The World
Creator	Creation
Heaven	earth
Spirit	matter
Life	death
Eternal	temporary

Since what we consider to be spiritual Truth forms the basis of our beliefs, it's the spiritual dimension we'll be looking into to find out why we believe.

Knowing Truth

How do we know that the Truth we seek is a matter of the spiritual dimension and not the physical world? We know, because in the physical world everything is changing.

So. . . does Truth change? No.

Are you changing? Yes. You're not the same person who sat down to read a few minutes ago. You're growing older as you read this. So you are not the Truth.

What you say goes, GOD, and stays, as permanent as the heavens. Your truth never goes out of fashion, it's as up-to-date as the earth when the sun comes up. Your Word and truth are dependable as ever, that's what you ordered — you set the earth going.
-Psalm 119:89-91, _The Message_

Is your chair changing? Yes. It's wearing out as you sit in it. So it's not the Truth.

Are you and I changing? Yes. So you and I together are not the Truth. Since you and I together are the church, the church is not the Truth. And no human institution is the Truth.

Does the world change? Yes. So this world and all of nature are not the Truth.

Does the form in which Truth is expressed change? Yes. So our forms — the Sabbath, circumcision, baptism, communion — are not the Truth.

Then how do we know what Truth is? The best way, though not the only way, is by the Spirit of Truth. So the confirmation of Truth is never what physical data may prove. Instead, the confirmation of Truth is always God's Spirit stirring in our spirits, telling us, "Yes. This is True."

The Bible is another witness to Truth. But what we read there is not Truth simply because it's in the Bible. Instead, it's in the Bible because it's Truth. We often see the Truth that's in the Bible and then say the Bible revealed that Truth to us. Actually, *God* revealed that Truth *through* the Bible. The revelation was not from the Bible itself, but from God. It is God who is Truth, the One who has all Knowledge and Wisdom, the One who does not change, the One who is permanent.

So Truth is not a what, but a Who.

Truth is God Himself.

So Truth was Truth long before the Bible was written.

Truth is deeper than the Bible.

Truth is older than the Bible.

Adam didn't have a Bible, but he knew Truth. Abraham, Isaac,

Jacob, and Joseph didn't have a Bible. But they knew Truth. Moses didn't have a Bible, but he knew Truth. In fact, when Moses went up the mountain in the desert, it was Truth who provided laws for him to bring back to the people so they would be able to form a civilized society that respected and followed Truth.

Even when Jesus came, people had no Bible as we know it. There were few copies of the writings they did have (our Old Testament), and many people couldn't read. Besides, what Jesus taught radically challenged how people understood the scriptures: "You have heard that the law of Moses says, 'Do not commit adultery,'" said Jesus. "But I say, anyone who even looks at a woman with lust in his eye has already committed adultery with her in his heart. . . . You have heard that the law of Moses says, 'Love your neighbor and hate your enemy.' But I say, love your enemies! Pray for those who persecute you! In that way, you will be acting as true children of your Father in heaven. For he gives his sunlight to both the evil and the good, and he sends rain on the just and on the unjust, too." [1]

The people Jesus taught had been living at head-level, checking off the rules they followed, thinking that those rules were Truth. Jesus pointed out that Truth goes deeper than rules. Truth is spiritual and is found only by looking to your spirit. That's where God's Spirit of Truth connects with people and confirms that what they are hearing, seeing, or thinking is really True.

Jesus didn't even count on miracles to show that He was bringing the Truth. Miracles helped people become aware that God was truly God and that Jesus was truly His Son. But many people who saw the miracles, including Jewish leaders, didn't believe. They saw physically, but they wouldn't listen to God's Spirit. So how did Jesus expect that people would know He was the Truth? He relied on the Spirit of God speaking to their spirits to confirm Truth. And that's exactly what happened. The crowds were amazed, because Jesus spoke like He knew what He was talking about.[2]

Just what had Jesus said? He had said that people are happiest when they are content with what they have, when they are hungry for more of God, when they care about others, when they make peace. He said people shouldn't worry, because if they are seeking God, He'll make sure they have all they need. [3] When Jesus taught, people heard nothing to argue about. They didn't need to compare what He said with any scripture. In their spirits they knew He was telling the Truth.

Even the officers who had been sent to arrest Jesus could hear the Truth of what He said. They returned empty-handed. The leaders asked, "Why didn't you arrest Him?" The officers said, "We never heard anyone speak the way this man does!"[4]

The two men who met Jesus on the road after He had risen from death said to each other, "Didn't our hearts burn within us as he talked to us?" The Spirit of Truth was telling their spirits that Jesus was speaking Truth. They described the feeling of that communication as a "burn."[5]

Jesus said, "I am the Truth." And "The Spirit of truth. . .will come to you from the Father and will tell you all about me." The apostle Paul wrote, "The Spirit himself testifies with our spirit. . ." Proof is spiritual, not physical.[6]

God has given every human the authority, the power and right, to know what is true and what is false, what is good and what is bad, what is beautiful and what is hideous. He asks people to decide Truth by listening to His voice within them. So deciding what's True is an individual, personal judgment that comes from the heart. That's because Truth, Beauty, and Goodness are above and beyond humans, from the spiritual dimension, a realm that's not proved by scientific instruments or historical facts. For Truth, Beauty, and Goodness are God, and He is not proved by physical tools. He is known in the spirit, and He has made it possible for us to identify Him with our spirits. In the next chapter, we'll use our spirits to start discovering the Truth, Beauty, and Goodness that we know we know. We'll explore how and why we know it. Because the final witness to Truth has to be your own honest, "Yes!" It has to be your spirit saying, "I know that I know."

They Said

They said I reached too high
    when I reached for the sky,
For my hand, it went straight through.
      But the other side was bathed in Light.
      Truth's heart was beating, fully alive.
      Drawing my gaze to the highest height.
And that's where I met You.

But some won't try
    to reach for the sky,
To reach for that One brilliant star,
      For their dreams have turned
      And crashed and burned
      Under the blows that they think they've earned.
And their hearts are hurt,
    So they think they've learned
That the sky is 'way too far.

They said I reached too high
    when I reached for the sky,
For my hand, it went straight through
      And punched a hole in the roof of night
      That let in a shining shaft of light.
      Though some would say that it's now too bright,
It greatly improved my view.

Where we are so far. . .

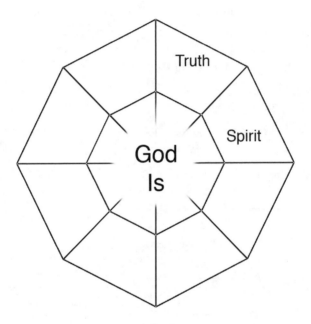

Chapter 3

It's a
Head-Gut
Thing

Remember your World History study of ancient Greece? Philosophers like Socrates and Plato would sit around all day on a hill in Athens and discuss ideas. People still do that, only now they meet at Starbucks or Portland Brew or Bongo Java. The ancient Greek philosophers called their way of discussing **dialogue**, because people would bounce ideas off each other and get everyone's thoughts on a matter. They were trying to figure out the world and themselves. Buddha, too, taught his followers by using dialogue. Even Jesus Himself taught this way.

The word "dialogue" comes from the Greek **dia**, which means "through," plus **logos**, which means "word" or "reason." So reasoning to truth "through words" is dialogue. There's another important word that comes from "logos": **logic**. Logic is when something makes sense. Like the type of reasoning you have to use in math:

If 2 + 2 = 4 and 3 + 1 = 4, then 2 + 2 = 3+ 1.

Logical.

So what does this have to do with anything? This is the head part of the head-gut thing. It's the part of thinking that figures things out so they make sense. Logic is, of course, very important to scientists, mathematicians, and other researchers, because they use this reasoning to arrive at proof for their theories. In their line of work, knowing something in your gut only gets you started. In the long run, it doesn't count for much unless it can be proved by logic. So logic and reasoning have been the popular way of talking and thinking for several centuries, even through the 20th century. Some people (especially people who lived most of their lives in the 20th century) still think and reason this way. It's one of the signs of a "modern" person. And, the truth is: Logic is still a valid way to think and reason.

But we are not living in "modern" times anymore. We live in a "post-modern" age. Even though we like to sit around and talk like the philosophers in Athens did, logic is not as important to post-modern people. Experience is important. Feeling is important. Being tuned-in to your spirit is important. An inner "knowing" is important. Beauty matters. Goodness matters. That's the gut part of the head-gut thing.

The Greeks had a word for *inner* knowledge: "splanchnon." That means "intestines" or "guts." We often refer to our feelings as coming from our "heart." But in Greek thought, feelings came from the gut. Instead of "I love you with all my heart," it would be "I love you with all my guts." Instead of "my heart tells me it's true," it's "my gut tells me it's true." Instead of breaking someone's heart, you might break someone's guts.

The point is, when we're talking about what we believe and why, we need to have a balance of both mind-logic and heart-knowledge. Both head and gut. So it's a head-gut thing.

For a long time, Christians have tried to reason everything out. And that's fine. Unless beliefs stay only at the head level. To be real and significant, our beliefs need to go beyond logic all the way to the heart. Or gut. We can get out of balance by putting the weight of our beliefs on logic only. And we can get out of balance by settling the weight of our beliefs on gut only. So in this book, you'll find both head and gut. Because logic is important, but Truth goes deeper than logic.

Dia-Logos

You are famous, GOD, for welcoming God-seekers, for decking us out in delight.

--Psalm 5:12
The Message

     Okay, let's do a little dialogue here. A little head-gut thing. We'll start with a very basic question. But first, one ground rule: It's not fair to answer by just saying what you think your parents want to hear (or your teacher or your youth pastor or your friends). You have to answer by what your gut tells you is true. Because if it's not true to you, then . . . it's not true to you. And if it's not true to you, you don't believe it. So be honest, okay? Here we go:

- Is there a God? What does your gut tell you? (You don't have to answer this yet, if you want to think about it.)

- If there is a God, is He greater than you, or less than you? By definition, a God is greater than a human. Is that what your gut tells you?

- If my assumptions are correct, then like most other humans, you think, feel, plan, create, remember, communicate. . . right?

- So if God is greater than you, then He has to at least think, feel, plan, create, remember, and communicate. Is that what your gut tells you?

- What is the highest, greatest feeling you can feel, the greatest concept you can think of? Most people say it's love. Is that what your gut tells you?

- What kind of love is the greatest? Think of some of the people the world says are the greatest human beings ever: Ghandi, Mother Theresa, the rescue workers of 9/11. Think of the most admired characters in books and movies, the characters who are heroes. What's the greatest act of giving and loving they do? They stand up for their friends. They defend those who are weak. They give up their lives to save someone else. Is that what your gut tells you?

- So if the greatest concept you can think of is self-sacrificial love, and if God is greater than you, then He has to be at least as great as the greatest concept you can think. He has to be at least as great as to know that giving His life for someone else is the greatest proof of His love. Is that what your gut tells you?

If There Were a God

Remember the student who asked my missionary friend Ken Rideout, "Is God playing games?" Here's another true story about someone who challenged Ken:

Ken was eating lunch with an Indonesian banker one day. The banker said, "I have lived a long time and have seen lots of evil in this world: killing, war, injustice, cruelty. In fact, right outside the door of this restaurant, there are people who don't have enough food to eat, and here we sit in luxury, enjoying ourselves. If there were a God, he would not create or tolerate a world like this. Therefore, I don't believe there's a God. If there were a God, he would not be worthy of my respect."

Ken took out a piece of paper and drew a line down the middle, making two columns. On the left, he wrote "The

World." Then he listed the evils for which the banker had accused God. On the other side, he wrote "God." Pointing to the chart, Ken repeated what the banker had just said, blaming God for allowing these terrible situations to exist in the world.

The World		God
Adultery	Stealing	
Lying	Rape	
Cheating	War	
Murder	Cruelty	

"Let's say that there is no God," said Ken. He drew an X through God's name in the right column. "Has anything changed now that we have taken God out of the picture?"

The World		~~God~~
Adultery	Stealing	
Lying	Rape	
Cheating	War	
Murder	Cruelty	

"No," said the banker.

"Without God in the picture, who is to blame for the evil that is in the world: the lying, stealing, cheating, murder, adultery, rape, war, and so forth?" asked Ken.

"People," said the banker.

Ken wrote "People" in the right column under the crossed-out "God."

The World		~~God~~
		PEOPLE
Adultery	Stealing	
Lying	Rape	
Cheating	War	
Murder	Cruelty	

"Why blame people for all the evil?" Ken asked. "The tiger eats the deer. The cat eats the mouse. A landslide wipes out an entire village. Why don't we blame the tiger, cat, and landslide in the same way we blame people?"

"Because people are responsible beings with wills," said the banker. "People choose their actions."

"Are you sure people are responsible?" Ken asked.

"Yes," said the banker.

"Then why blame God for what you say people have freely chosen to do?" asked Ken. "If people are responsible for choosing to do evil, we might as well put God back in the picture. It seems like God may be people's only hope to get out of the mess they've made of life."

People may deny the existence of God or blame Him for the state the world is in, but as this Chinese banker had to admit, the problem is really people themselves.

So is there a God? What does your head tell you? Does your gut agree?

> *"The worst moment for the atheist is when he is really thankful and has nobody to thank."*
> — *Dante Gabriel Rossetti, poet and painter, England* [1]

Getting Personal

But is God personal or impersonal? In other words, is He a living being, or is He simply a life-force, an essence of energy?

Think about Mother Theresa for a minute. Most people would say that she showed self-sacrificial love. Why would they say that? Is it because she sat around all day with her eyes closed, thinking *love, love, love*? Think about the rescue workers on 9/11. Were they watching CNN, thinking *love, love, love*?

def of personal?

Of course not. Mother Theresa cared for the poor, sick, and dying in India by providing food and shelter and clothing and kind words. The rescue workers of 9/11 ran into crumbling buildings to help people escape. They carried people and fought fires and even gave their lives in the process. Love is active, giving, merciful.

But love cannot exist by itself. If someone says, "I love," it doesn't mean much. But if they say, "I love you," then *that* means something. Love must have something to which it gives itself. It must have someone to help. Someone to encourage.

So love itself is not impersonal. Instead, love is shared from person to person. That's one thing that identifies humans as personal, living, rational beings: They love.

God = love.

Back to our dialogue:

If there's a God, He's greater than the greatest concept we can think of. . . which is love.

Love is personal and must have something to give itself to.

So if God is love, then God is personal and must have something to give Himself to.

And that something is us. Human beings.

We don't have to prove any of this; we know it in our guts. Or if you prefer: We know it in our spirits. Same thing. Remember: God's Spirit confirms Truth to our spirits. If it's true, we don't need to prove it. We simply *know* that we know.

Notice something very important here: We have done a head-gut scan of what you believe and why. But we have not used the Bible to prove anything. There's a reason for that: You cannot prove the Bible. Sure, you can go to historical records and talk about manuscripts and what scholars say. But remember the true stories from the first chapter? If someone asks you why you believe in God, and you say, "Because the Bible says God exists," their next question is likely to be, "Why do you believe the Bible?"

Then you're into trying to explain what the scholars say, and you end up shrugging and saying, "You just have to take it on faith." And then your friend says, "Well, I'm glad that works for you. But I'm into Zen."

Truth is what you know you know, and it's Truth whether or not you have a Bible in your hand, and whether or not you even mention the Bible. Truth was true even before the Bible was ever written. Remember: It's not Truth simply because it's in the Bible. It's in the Bible because it's Truth. Yes, from cover to cover, the Bible is full of Truth. The Bible helps to mature and perfect your faith. But what and why you believe is not based on the Bible. Your belief goes much deeper than that. Your gut belief goes all the way back to before the beginning of time, when a God, who is greater than your highest thought of love, chose to display His love in a world populated with human beings who could receive His love and give it to each other as well.

How did God do that? It's all a matter of image, as we'll see in the next chapter.

Chapter 4

Becoming Image-Conscious

Are you image-conscious? Do you dress a certain way, act a certain way, go to certain places, have certain friends, all to portray a certain image to the world around you? Most people do. Movie stars, politicians, and other famous people are so image-conscious that they often hire image consultants who tell them how to dress and where to go and who to meet so that the public will perceive them in just the way the famous person wants.

God is image-conscious too. The difference is, people try to hide the less desirable parts of their bodies and personalities, and enhance the more attractive parts. So the images that people display are false in some way. But God has nothing to hide. He displays His image with complete honesty, showing who He is, revealing His generosity, His grace, and His love. (That's what *glory* means: showing who God is. But more about that later.)

In fact, as far back as human memory and recorded history can reach, there was God, revealing Himself. You know the biblical account: darkness lay upon the face of the earth. God then created sky and earth and seas. But there was no awareness of God. Not in the trees. Not in the rocks. There was no one to experience the beauty of it all. The giving of love was not complete, because love exists only where there is life and awareness. The greatest thing God could do was to recreate His love. So God created human beings, and wrote His love into their hearts. Love that had freedom. Love that had creative power. This was the crowning act of God's work: creating a being who contained His image.

> "So God created people in His own image,
> God . . .formed a man's body from the dust of
> the ground and breathed into it the breath of life.
> And the man became a living person."[1]

When God did this, He placed the identical image of Love into all human beings, no matter what race, creed, belief, or nationality they might be. That means God has not put a different image into the Asian people from the image that He put into the African or the Native American or the Chinese or the Arab or the Northern European. Everyone on this planet has been created with one identical image: God's. This identity unifies humanity.

From math, you know that in order to add fractions like $1/3 + 5/6$, you have to first find a common denominator. $1/3 = 2/6$, so $2/6 + 5/6 = 1\ 1/6$. It's similar with human relationships. If we find a common denominator among people, it unites people. Among all human beings, God's image of Love is the common denominator by which all of us can:

identify Truth,

confirm God's heart and character,

and come together as humans on this planet.

This Kind of Love

This common denominator of Love expresses human beings' total uniqueness compared to all other creatures. Every human being knows, gut-level, that love binds us together: mother with child, husband with wife, friend with friend. All of us know that a person who loves will try to make things better for others. A person who loves will work toward whatever will bring life. A beautiful, deep, full life. So Love, our Maker's image, placed in us by our Maker, is the common image in all people.

Now: Is this kind of love good or bad? (Yes, it's a strange question, but that proves that the answer is a Truth that everyone knows in their gut. And because we're doing the head-gut thing here, it's important to establish this fact.)

Hmmm. . .if love is *good*, then we have moved into the area of morality: good and evil.

If our Maker has placed His image in each human, and
- if His image within us is Love, and
- if Love is morally good,
- then God's image of Love within humans is the Standard for morality.

If that's true, then *all* people should have a common sense of right and wrong. In other words, in their gut, everyone should know a natural standard of morality, a basic sense of right and wrong. Let's see if that's true. What does your gut tell you in answer to the following questions?

Is it right for me to murder you?

Is it right for me to steal from you?

Is it right for me to rape you?

Is it right for me to deceive you or cheat you?

Do you have to prove that your answers here are right?

No matter what people's age, race, nationality, or religion (even if they are atheist), everyone answers these questions the same way: *No.* Why? It's a Truth that we humans know we know. (Some people might rationalize that it would be all right to steal from someone else, but when you ask them if it's right for someone to steal from *them*, they say no.)

Next question: If I loved you perfectly, would I murder you, steal from you, rape you, deceive you, or cheat you?

Again, everyone answers *No* to this question. Why? It's a Truth that people know they know. Why? Because of God's image in us, God's Love in us.

What kind of world would it be if everyone loved perfectly?

We all know the answer. All people know that if we encourage, understand, and help others, we express the Love that is moral Truth.

So within each heart, God's image, His Love, is the standard for our relationships with each other. Even if people don't believe in God, they know that Perfect Love is the highest goal to aim for. And they sense that if there were a God, the most important Truth would be that God loves them and that there is hope for all humanity. We don't have to prove any of this. Our gut tells us it's True.

Burnished Bronze

Oh burnished bronze,
Oh child of fire
flaming up in Me
if you only knew
how close I am,
you'd never fret or fear.
I in you and you in Me.
The mystery is mine,
but the facts are yours:
you could not be any
closer.

I am in you.

Another point about Love: Its nature is to stay in relationship and to communicate. God, being perfect Love, stays in relationship and communicates with the humans He created. Now God doesn't speak English. Or I should say, God doesn't speak *only* English. (He *can*, of course, speak English any time He wants. It's just that English is not His primary language.) God's native language is Spirit. Because God is a Spirit Being. So when we say that our gut tells us that something is True, what we really mean is that God's Spirit is confirming Truth to our spirits. God communicates with everyone, because everyone is made in His image. The very fact that God's image of Love is in every person means that there is constant communication to each person's gut telling him or her that Perfect Love is the moral Standard: be kind, share, help, encourage, etc. Of course, it's one thing to have that communication within you, and it's totally another thing to choose to *listen* to it.

You may have noticed something very interesting about God. He doesn't limit Himself to speaking only to people whom we would traditionally call "God's people." Check your Bible for this. God spoke through King Cyrus, Balaam, and King Nebuchadnezzar. None of them were Hebrews, "God's people." God spoke to Cornelius, a Roman. Through Jesus, He spoke to a Roman centurion, a Syro-Phoenician woman, and a Samaritan woman. At that time only Jews were considered to be "God's people." But for all of these non-Jews, their "copy" of the image of God within them confirmed the Truth.[2]

> *Is there anyplace I can go to avoid your Spirit? to be out of your sight? If I climb to the sky, you're there! If I go underground, you're there! If I flew on morning's wings to the far western horizon, You'd find me in a minute — you're already there waiting!*
> - Psalm 139:7-10, The Message

So by creating all humans in His image, God placed a knowledge of Himself within each of them. People don't have to seek God in some far-off place. He made all of us in His image so that we can know Him. This makes all humans one by giving us a common denominator, a common Standard: His image of Love within us. So anytime *anyone* sees or experiences joy, peace, patience, kindness, gentleness, goodness, faithfulness, self-control, or any other attribute of Love, they are seeing and experiencing God's image.

Now you might think that if people of all ethnic groups and nationalities have the image of God within them, they'd be seeking God or Perfect Love or whatever they sense this image is. If that's what you think, you're right. Stay tuned for more details.

"For you there is no reality that is closer to God than yourself."
—*Anthony De Mello*[3]

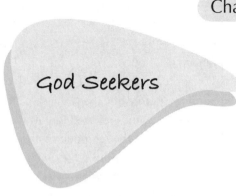

Chapter 5

God Seekers

Most humans want the best life they can get. We work toward achieving the most health, peace, joy, comfort, beauty, whatever we think will make life better. We sense that if there is such a thing as health, then there must be such a thing as perfect health somewhere. If there is such a thing as peace, there must be perfect peace somewhere. There must be perfect joy, perfect comfort, perfect beauty. Why would we sense this? Because we are all created in the image of Perfect Love. God has placed His image within each of us.

From ancient times to today, the image of God within people has stirred them to express that image, describe it, find a name for it. Let's go back to ancient Greece, about 600 years before Jesus was born. Remember that these Greeks had no Bible, no Scriptures, no Ten Commandments. But they knew in their gut (or spirit, if you prefer) that they were not the highest intelligence in the universe. They understood that reality existed in two dimensions: the seen and the unseen (or the physical and spiritual, or the temporary and permanent). They sensed the life-force of God, and spoke of Him as the Divine Essence, the creative power that creates and governs everything.

About the same time in history, but in a different part of the world, Buddhism was born. To Buddha, the highest level a person could reach would be completely without anything earthly. He called this level "Nirvana." But even before Buddha, Hinduism developed. For Hindus, the Essence was the unreachable, unapproachable, out-of-this-world, transcendental level called Supreme Brahman. The Chinese called the Essence the Unnamed, and sometimes referred to it as the Tao (pronounced "Dow"). So even though none of these groups had the Bible, the Jewish Scriptures, or the Ten Commandmants, they were all searching for God, listening to that gut-feeling that there was someone or something Great and Beautiful and Excellent and far beyond them.

Not only have humans tried to describe and express the Essence, but they also have tried to discover how to achieve a union or harmony with their concept of this highest level. So for thousands of years, people have searched for a mediator. *Mediator* comes from the word *middle*. A mediator is someone who gets into the middle of a conflict in order to help both sides come to peace. In the case of the Divine Essence, humans realized that they needed a mediator to go between themselves and whatever their concept of the Essence was. Their thoughts and ideas about a mediator are part of today's global culture, which as a whole accepts many beliefs and many views about God and spiritual life. So as we take a closer look, notice how each of these particular views tries to reach and relate to the Divine Essence.

The Logos

In the centuries before Jesus came, Greek philosophers were puzzling over how finite humans could reach into the infinite Essence of God's goodness. They wondered how an all-knowing God could have a relationship with a wicked world.

When my heart whispered, "Seek God," my whole being replied, "I'm seeking him!"
— Psalm 27:8, *The Message*

They came up with the concept of *Logos*, which we have already seen means "word" or "reason." To them, *Logos*
expressed God's mysterious Essence
revealed what was hidden
guided them to knowledge
taught what was right and good
held powerful cosmic creativity
formed a bridge between humans and the Creator,
but was IMPERSONAL (not a person).[1]

Jesus' friend John understood the way the Greeks thought. So when he wrote, he used the Greek word *Logos*. Here's an English version with the Greek word dropped back in:

In the beginning was the *Logos*, and the *Logos* was with God and the *Logos* was God. . . .In him was life, and the life was the light of all people . . . .the true light that enlightens every-one.[2]

What John is saying is, "I'm going to tell you about what you call *Logos*. Your definition of Logos is right, except the Logos is PERSONAL. Logos is not a concept; Logos is a Being. He is the One who expresses God's mysterious Essence, who reveals what is hidden, who guides us to knowledge, who teaches what is right and good, who holds powerful cosmic cre-ativity, who forms a bridge between humans and the Creator. I have seen Him, and I can tell you that He is alive. He is the One who enlightens all people."

So the Greeks were looking for a way to be in harmony with God. John said, "I'll tell you about Him."

The Dhamma

Like the Logos, dhamma is a mysterious guide. According to Buddhist teaching, when Buddha received his enlightenment, it was the dhamma that enlightened him. Dhamma:

is the law of nature,

teaches about right conduct,

is sometimes described as the law of karma (actions and consequences),

can also mean ultimate reality or universal Truth

is the raft that takes a person to Nirvana.[3]

So Buddhists, too, were describing something that enlightens and becomes a raft or bridge that enables them to reach the highest level possible. What does John show in his writing? The One who enlightens the world. In fact, the Bible translation from Sri Lanka, a strongly Buddhist country, uses *dhamma* in John chapter 1 to mean the Word, the *Logos*.

In the beginning was the *dhamma*, and the *dhamma* was with God and the *dhamma* was God. . . the true light that enlightens everyone.

In other words, "In the beginning was the raft that takes you to the highest level you can reach. He teaches about right conduct toward others. He is the ultimate reality, the universal Truth. He is the true light that enlightens everyone."

The Brahman

To Hindus, the highest level was the Supreme Brahman, which they saw as a pure consciousness everywhere in the universe but existing outside it, just as the sun spreads through all

life on earth but exists outside earth's realm. Supreme Brahman
is the cause of the universe,

> from which all things come,
>> free from limits of time and space,
>> by which all are supported,
>>> and into which all finally disappear.

The ultimate purpose of a Hindu life is to reach this Supreme
Brahman, and Hindus want to communicate somehow with this
great unapproachable Reality. That's where the second level
comes in, the *conditioned* Brahman who has physical features.

Hindus believe they can commmunicate with the conditioned Brahman, who becomes the bridge between them and the
unapproachable Supreme Brahman. They say the conditioned
Brahman is the all-powerful, all-knowing Creator, Preserver, and
Destroyer of the world. They often call the conditioned
Brahman "Lord" or "God." And they believe that one way that
the conditioned Brahman works is that when necessary, it can
manifest itself as a man for awhile. When this happens, the conditioned Brahman is called the Avatar.[4]

These ideas are what Hindu thinkers came up with
when they, too, searched for the way to get to God.

> *The main thing to remember here is that Lao Tze
> and the Taoists, like the Greek philosophers, Buddhists,
> and Hindus were searching for a way to know God.*

The Tao

Lao Tze (born between 570 - 604 B.C.) was the Chinese
philosopher who came up with the concept of the Tao which
grew into the religion of Taoism. Lao Tze himself found it hard
to say exactly what the Tao is. For one thing, he says the Tao of

the universe is an eternal cosmic energy which brings about order and harmony in heaven and earth. But literally, Tao means "way" or "road," so it's also a system or method of living.[5]

However, Lao Tze identified the Tao with God:

> There exists a Being undifferentiated and complete,
> Born before Heaven and earth
> Tranquil, boundless,
> Abiding alone and changing not,
> Encircling everything with exhaustion
> Fathomless, it seems to be the Source of all things.
> But characterize it as the Tao,
> Arbitrarily forcing a name upon it,
> I call it Great.   (Tao Te Ching 25:1-2)

So the Tao is a "logos-like" word for the bridge to reach God. In fact, in John 1 in the Chinese Bible, the word *Logos* is translated *Tao*.

> In the beginning was the *Tao*,
> and the *Tao* was with God
> and the *Tao* was God. . .

In other words, "In the beginning was the One who is complete, the One who lived before Heaven and earth, the One who is tranquil and boundless, the One who abides alone and does not change, the One who encircles everything, the One who is the Source of all things. He was in the beginning with God, and He was God."

The main thing to remember here is that Lao Tze and the Taoists, like the Greek philosophers, Buddhists, and Hindus were searching for a way to know God.

The Torah

The authority and guide for Jewish worship and life is the Torah, their "instruction." They see God, whom they called YHWH (Yah'weh or Yeh ho weh) as personal, but unapproachable. He is the One who made covenant with them and spoke to them through the Torah, the law. For them, the law is what bridges the gap between humans and God. So as they seek God, they try to approach Him through obeying the law, the Torah.

The Qur'an of Islam

Greek philosophers, Hinduism, and Buddhism were around long before Jesus was born. But Islam arose hundreds of years *after* the birth of Jesus, and it's quite different from the other religions and philosophies. Islam was started by a man named Mohammed, whom Muslims deeply revere as the final prophet of God, even though they point out that he was nothing more than a man.

As you probably know, Muslims call God "Allah." They also believe Jesus lived, but as a prophet of God, not as God's Son. Islam requires people to strictly obey the Qur'an, their sacred scriptures. They believe the Qur'an contains the very words of God and guides them in all areas of life. But much of the Qur'an treats ritual, ceremony, and culture as equal to the Truth itself.[6] So for Muslims, as for other religions, their way of life is bound up in obeying rules and law in order to win favor and reward from Allah.

* * * * * * * *

In any religion, ritual and tradition can be *expressions* of the Truth. But rituals and traditions have no *eternal* value. Remember the two dimensions. Eternal Truth never changes. So only God is eternal Truth. Any religion, sect, or denomination is on dangerous ground when it elevates its rituals and traditions to a place that equals the Truth Himself. When that happens, the people who follow those beliefs usually start thinking that everyone else should follow their rituals and traditions. They then find it hard to have mercy, compassion, and tolerance for people who *don't* follow their rituals and traditions. The rituals and traditions become the rules by which they live as well as the standard for them to say who's "in" and who's "out," who's accepted by God and who's not. As we'll see, rules (law) are impersonal,

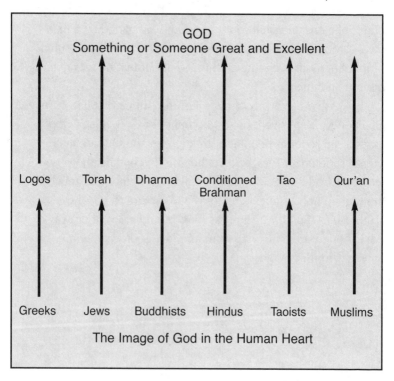

GOD
Something or Someone Great and Excellent

| Logos | Torah | Dharma | Conditioned Brahman | Tao | Qur'an |

| Greeks | Jews | Buddhists | Hindus | Taoists | Muslims |

The Image of God in the Human Heart

so they can't have mercy or forgive. Those who focus only on their religion's rules, rituals, and traditions tend to be the same. They find it hard to forgive. Many of them resort to "an eye for an eye and a tooth for a tooth," which can become a

Like it or not, we all have karma

cycle of revenge. That's the darkest side of what karma can become. Where do we find the most fighting (verbally and physically) in the world today? Among groups who hold rituals and traditions as the standard instead of holding Love as the Standard.

These descriptions of philosophies and religions are general, of course. And these are not the only philosophies and religions in the world. But from this quick scan, we can see that all people know in their gut that there is a spiritual dimension to life, and that there is a Great One in charge of it all. Some people refuse to listen to that gut knowledge. But most people seek God. They dialogue. They formulate their thoughts and share their teachings. We can understand that. We seek God too. We dialogue. We formulate our thoughts and share our teachings.

Then why do you believe what you do? Why aren't you Buddhist or Hindu or Taoist? What makes you think that what you believe is any better than what they believe?

These are very important questions, and only you can answer these questions for yourself. So let's keep dialoguing about human spirituality, because all of us humans are orbiting the sun together. And we all have something in common: the image of God, His Love, His Truth within us.

There's something else we all have in common: karma. Like it or not, we all have karma. But that's a subject for the next chapter.

Where we are so far. . .

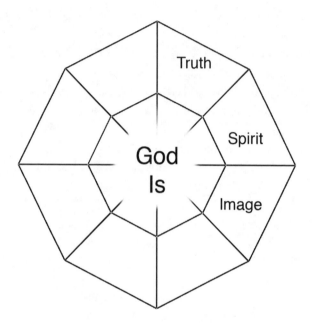

Good Karma

Bad Karma

The whole physical world is controlled and ordered by natural laws. We're not talking about speed limit laws or voting-age laws or any other people-made laws here. We're talking about natural laws, the limits within which the world works. You learned about these when you studied math and physics and other sciences: the law of gravity, Archimedes' principle, Newton's laws of motion. These, of course, are not rules that anyone made up, but are just the way the world works.

Laws are simply cause and effect principles. Everything within nature follows the law of its own nature, whether it's animal, plant, or human. So the law of nature for a pig is different from the law of nature for a fish. In other words, **the law of anything is written within the thing itself**. For example, the law of the water lily is defined by the nature of the water lily. If you plant a water lily in dirt as if it were a rose, it dies. But if you plant a water lily in water, it thrives.

Laws make things predictable. That is, once there is a cause, an effect must follow it. For example, if the stem of an apple breaks loose from its branch, the apple must fall. By the same law of gravity, if a man jumps off a cliff, his jump will be the cause that will result in an immediate and deadly effect. Isaac Newton's famous Third Law of Motion states that every action causes an equal and opposite reaction. That's the cause and effect relationship of the physical world.

For as long as people have existed, they have been discovering these laws of nature. To discover the law of something is to understand how it works. And when we understand how something works, we can control it and use it. For example, by understanding how light works under a variety of circumstances, we can use light and organize our lives according to its nature. By observing cause and effect, doctors can prescribe medicines and treatments that help their patients. After centuries of observing and documenting laws of aerodynamics, astronauts were able to travel into space.

No one can escape natural law. We're controlled by it. We learn from it. We depend on it. But we can't make or change it. The only thing we can do is share what we've discovered about how it works. The law of nature seems to say, "Discover me. Use me to help. Or use me to harm. But you cannot change me." If we can't change a law of nature, our only choices are to accept it or reject it. If we reject a law of nature (the law of gravity or the law of electricity, for example), it gives us its own consequence.

The Law of Human Nature

The law of *human* nature operates in the same way as the natural laws of the physical world: by cause and effect. There are lots of ways to say this: "Garbage in, garbage out." Or "What goes around comes around." (Meaning, "The way you treat others is the way you'll be treated.") Or "You get back what you put out." Or "You reap what you sow." It all adds up to *karma*: You do good; good things happen to you. You do bad; bad things happen to you. People have known this principle since ancient times. You can guess why: Everyone has been created in God's image. So His image, Perfect Love, is the

"One touch of nature makes the whole world kin."
— *Shakespeare* [1]

Standard that everyone knows in their gut they should live up to. It's the natural *moral* law written on our hearts.

When my friend Ken first went to Asia, he thought he had to teach people the moral law: Don't lie, don't murder, don't steal. He was surprised to learn that Buddhism had been teaching morality for 2500 years. Buddhism emphasizes the importance of doing good deeds and thinking good thoughts. It tells people to get rid of all greed, hatred, and selfishness. It encourages compassion, joy, and calmness. It says, "Hatred ceases not by hatred in this world. Through love it comes to an end. This is an ancient law." And "Overcome anger by love, evil by good. Conquer the greedy with liberality and with truth the speaker of falsehoods."[2]

How could Buddhists come up with something so similar to our way of thinking? They figured it out, because they were created in God's image, Perfect Love. Everyone knows in their gut that Perfect Love will not be greedy or selfish, and that it will have compassion and joy.

> *Let me give you some good advice, I'm looking you in the eye and giving it to you straight:*
>
> *Don't be ornery like a horse or mule that needs bit and bridle to stay on track."*
>
> *God-defiers are always in trouble;*
>
> *God-affirmers find themselves loved every time they turn around.*
>
> — Psalm 32:8-10, *The Message*

Just as physical laws are not made but discovered, so also moral law is discovered — within us. All the philosophies and religions of the world get their moral principles by discovering laws of human nature. Buddhism, Taoism, Confucianism, Hinduism and other religions have been teaching "do good, do good, do good" for thousands of years. And remember the Greek philosophers? They said that divine law was the foundation of society and moral conduct.[3] Later, the Romans used these same Greek ideas to develop their own principles of moral law. In China, the Confucian philosopher Mencius traveled for years at a time teaching principles of cause and effect, focusing on the fact that the knowledge of right and wrong is inborn in humans and that wisdom will follow what's right.

"Two things fill me with constantly increasing admiration and awe, the longer and more earnestly I reflect on them: the starry heavens without and the moral law within."
   — *Immanuel Kant, German philosopher*[4]

Just to make sure we understand the point clearly, let's look at it this way. Being aware of the Standard, Perfect Love, which is the image of God within,

Buddhists formulated the dhamma. . . .
   . . . telling the way to live. Rules. Law. Karma.

Hindus formulated the Conditioned Brahman. . .
   . . . telling the way to live. Rules. Law. Karma.

Lao Tze developed the Tao (Way). . .
   . . . telling the Way to live. Rules. Law. Karma.

Islam embraced the Qur'an. . .
   . . . telling the way to live. Rules. Law. Karma.

Confucianism had its principles. . .
   . . . telling the way to live. Rules. Law. Karma.

Judaism received their Torah, including the Ten Commandments. . .
   . . . telling the way to live. Rules. Law. Karma.

Christians take the Torah, the teachings of Jesus, and the apostles' letters. . . . . telling the way to live. And many of us see them as Rules. Law. Karma.

Rules-Law-Karma

So what are all these rules-law-karma? In a byte: "do good, do good, do good." Because that's what Love does. Perfect Love achieves the Standard, because Perfect Love *is* the Standard. God. He's the yardstick by which all behavior is measured, the goal, the mark, the bull's eye of the target.

So "do good" and "be loving." These rules sound wonderful. Godly. Right. And they are. Because they come from the image of God, Perfect Love, the Standard, the natural moral law within all people. And since law is simply cause and effect (karma), you do good and you get good in return. You share, and others share with you. Simple. All we have to do is love in all situations like God does. Then we'll live up to the Standard. Good karma. So far so good.

There's just one problem:
Nobody has ever been able to love perfectly.
Nobody.
Ever.

So what happens if you slip up and *don't* share (either by accident or just because you happened to be feeling a bit ornery)? What if you're greedy or selfish — even just once? Bad karma. Then. . .

Cause must have an effect.
The action must have a consequence.
So bad things will happen to you as a consequence.
(Funeral music comes in right here.)

What bad things? Well, you get back what you put out. According to Buddhism and Hinduism and others who believe in rebirth or reincarnation, you may not pay for bad karma in this life, but your karma will be reborn or you will be reincarnated into a life in which you will pay for your previous bad karma. For example, in your next life, you might be born a leper. There's nothing you can do about it except live out your bad karma. And few people will feel like helping you, either. Why should they interfere with the consequences you are experiencing because of your past life?

On the other hand, those who don't believe in rebirth or reincarnation still know there are negative consequences for bad karma. You yell at someone, you damage the relationship. They may yell back at you, or tell someone you like how rude you are, or decide not to invite you to the party. Or ten years from now you need a job and, oops, that person is the boss who decides not to hire you.

Then again, maybe the person forgives you for yelling at them. Even then, your bad karma has reinforced your own immaturity. Worst of all, it has distanced you from God. The goal of "do good, do good, do good" was to move closer to God, right? So bad karma defeats the whole purpose of the dhamma, the Tao, the Conditioned Brahman, the Torah, the Qur'an, and Christian Law.

"For the sin they do by two and two they must pay for one by one."
-Rudyard Kipling, British author[5]

The simple fact is: You break the law, you pay the price. Buddhists know that. Hindus know that. Taoists know that. Muslims know that. Jews know that. *Everybody* knows that, gut-level. Remember, it's the same way with the laws of nature. If you step off a cliff, the law of gravity doesn't say, "Oops! I know you weren't watching where you were going. So I'll just forgive that little misstep, and we'll pretend it didn't happen." Nope. There's a consequence.

And so it is with natural moral law. No matter what a

religion calls the laws, the standards, the principles its origina-
tors discovered, under law (karma) there is no mercy. Why?
Because law is simple cause and effect. The effect must follow
the cause. Buddhism says: "It is absolutely impossible for a
conscious being to escape this result of his own act or thought,
or. . . his karma." [6]

Law is impersonal. It cannot forgive. People harvest
what they plant. That's just the way it is. That's law. That's
karma. And every human being experiences it.

It's getting awfully dark and stuffy in here. Anybody got
a light?

Look at that guy!
He had sex with sin,
he's pregnant with evil.
Oh, look! He's having
the baby — a Lie-Baby!

See that man shoveling day after day,
digging, then concealing, his man-trap
down that lonely stretch of road?
Go back and look again--
you'll see him in it headfirst,
legs waving in the breeze.
That's what happens:
mischief backfires,
violence boomerangs.

Psalm 7:14-16,
The Message

Where we are so far. . .

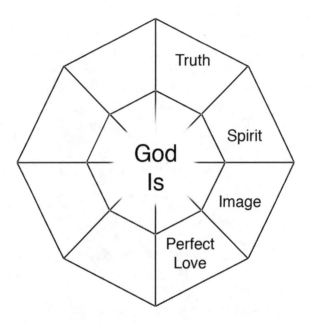

Chapter 7

Guilt-Colored Glasses

Now the serpent was more crafty than any of the wild animals the Lord God had made. He said to the woman, "Did God really say, 'You must not eat from any tree of the garden'?"

The woman said to the serpent, "We may eat fruit from the trees in the garden, but God did say, 'You must not eat fruit from the tree that is in the middle of the garden, and you must not touch it, or you will die.'"

"You will not surely die," the serpent said to the woman. "For God knows that when you eat of it your eyes will be opened, and you will be like God, knowing good and evil."

When the woman saw that the fruit of the tree was good for food and pleasing to the eye, and also desirable for gaining wisdom, she took some and ate it. She also gave some to her husband, who was with her, and he ate it. Then the eyes of both of them were opened. . . .

> Then the man and his wife heard the
> sound of the Lord God as he was walking in
> the garden in the cool of the day, and they
> hid from the Lord God among the trees of
> the garden.
>
> But the Lord God called to the man,
> "Where are you?" He answered, "I heard
> you in the garden, and I was afraid. . ."
>
> And he said, ". . . Have you eaten from
> the tree that I commanded you not to eat
> from?"
>
> The man said, "The woman you put
> here with me — she gave me some fruit
> from the tree, and I ate it."
>
> ---Genesis 3:1-12, NIV

Talk about bad karma! Knowing God, seeing Him, being right there in His presence, but disobeying anyway, then trying to wiggle out of the responsibility! Ouch! Let's wander around inside this story for a few minutes. We might find something interesting here.

When God left Adam and Eve in the morning, they had a loving relationship with their Maker. By the time God returned in the cool of the day, the relationship had changed. But who had changed? Not God. He was still the same loving, merciful, good Creator that He had been that morning. It was Adam and Eve who had changed. They were ashamed and afraid. Why? They had disobeyed.

It wasn't just that they had eaten a forbidden fruit. It was what the eating of the fruit represented: They had created a new *self* image, an image that opposed God: "My will against your will." They hadn't lived up to the Standard of Perfect Love placed in their hearts when God first created them.

A Distorted Point of View

Something else had changed, though: their perception of God. They could no longer perceive God as loving and good. They had known before, at head-level, that they held the freedom to make choices and exercise their own wills. But now they knew that their choices had tremendous, dangerous power. They had acquired a knowledge of good and evil. Now they knew that they could choose to oppose God. And when they made that choice, they became aware, gut-level, that they had fallen far short of the goal line.

Imagine a football player with the ball, sprinting toward a touchdown. But he trips and falls dropping the ball at the 20-yard line. He knows immediately that he didn't make it. Why? Because he can see the goal line, and he didn't get there. It's not the fault of the goal line. The goal line is not condemning him or telling him that he's blown it. Still, he may feel a sense of guilt or condemnation or anger.

Imagine that you are in an art class, learning to paint landscapes. You are a beginner. Your class is meeting outdoors. Everyone sets up their easels and canvases, and you all spend the morning painting the scene in front of you. When classtime is over, your teacher instructs you to line the paintings up side by side so everyone can view their classmates' work. Your painting sits beside Claude M's. He happens to be the best, most highly acclaimed landscape painter in the world. You had no idea until this moment. But your painting looks like a toddler's scribblings next to his, and you want to fade into the sunset. Why? Nobody is denouncing your painting. But you have suddenly seen the standard, and you automatically measure yourself by it.

That's kind of what happened to Adam and Eve.

Suddenly they saw the Standard of Perfect Love, because their action had come so short of that Standard that it was truly a no-brainer: Gut-level, they knew they had messed up. What had been simple, pure Love now became law to them, because they saw what they would have to DO to achieve it: do good, do good, do good. And now they knew that it wasn't as easy as it sounded.

Adam and Eve also knew, gut-level, that there should be a negative consequence for what they had done. What they had planted, they would have to harvest, and they could see no such thing as mercy. They knew that God, too, had the power of choice. So, assuming that God would choose not to forgive, they became afraid of Him. They ran and hid.

Did you ever do something you knew your parents would not approve of, but your parents didn't know you did it? And when you saw your parents, you had a hard time looking them in the eye? Maybe you felt yourself getting a little red in the face? Or hot? Or nervous? Your parents weren't angry at you, but you still distanced yourself from them.

> "Though the dungeon, the scourge, and the executioner be absent, the guilty mind can apply the goad and scorch with blows."
>
> — Lucretius, Roman poet and philosopher[1]

That's the way it was with Adam and Eve. They were seeing God through guilt-colored glasses that distorted their view of Him. His Love and beauty dimmed in their eyes because of their shame and fear. Think about it: To someone who's full of joy, a dark, rainy day can seem beautiful. To someone who is full of shame, a sunny day can seem depressing. The problem is not the weather, the problem is the condition of the person's heart. Adam and Eve saw God as angry and unforgiving, because they knew they had not lived up to His Perfect Love.

The View Through Guilt-Colored Glasses

Earth wobbles and lurches,
      huge mountains shake like leaves,
Quake like aspen leaves
      because of his rage.
His nostrils flare, bellowing smoke,
      his mouth spits fire.
Tongues of fire dart in and out,
      he lowers the sky.
He steps down,
      under his feet an abyss opens up.
He's riding a winged creature,
      swift on wind-wings.
Now he's wrapped himself
      in a trenchcoat of black-cloud darkness.
But his cloud-brightness bursts through,
      spraying hailstones and fireballs.
Then GOD thundered out of heaven,
      the High God gave a great shout,
      spraying hailstones and fireballs.
God shoots his arrows — pandemonium!
      He hurls his lightnings — a rout!
The secret sources of ocean are exposed,
      the hidden depths of earth lie uncovered.
The moment you roar in protest,
      let loose your hurricane anger.

— Psalm 18:7-15, The Message

Knowing Good and Evil

The relationship Adam and Eve had experienced with God was now replaced by a relationship with law (karma, cause and effect). Humans saw karma (law) as the mediator that would take them to harmony with God: If they could be good enough, they could measure up to the Standard and win God's favor. But it was impossible to be good enough. Having created a new self-image, and having tasted the power of sinful choice, Adam and Eve dug themselves deeper and deeper into bad karma.

As they "multiplied and filled the earth," people still had God's image in them. They still knew they should do good. But they just couldn't stop choosing evil. Instead, they invented new wrongs. By the time the book of Genesis has finished telling us the story of humanity's beginnings, we've read about murder, envy, war, jealousy, revenge, hatred, slavery, and more.

Here's something else to consider: Did God know Adam and Eve would eat the fruit from the tree of the knowledge of good and evil?

Think of it this way: If you are taking care of a two-year-old, and you show that two-year-old a beautiful red lollipop, then you set it within his reach and say to him, "Don't eat that lollipop; don't even touch it," what will the two-year-old do? As soon as you turn away, he'll go for the lollipop. You're smart enough to know that will happen. You don't set something in front of a toddler if you don't want him to have it. Are you smarter than God? I don't think so. So why did God set something in front of humans that He didn't want them to have?

God knew what Adam and Eve would do. In fact, he planned it. He set it all up by giving humans the right to control their own thoughts, intentions, and decisions. God gave humans free will. Choice. But we can't exercise choice unless there's something to choose.

Still, how did God know that people would choose to disobey instead of obey? He knew, because humans are not God. It's a simple fact that humans can never live all the time being as perfectly good as their Maker. When God decided to put the knowledge of His infinite Love in people, He knew that no one could live up to that Standard of Love. Humans are the creation and not the Creator.

God, of course, does not do wrong. How could He? He's the Standard. So whatever He does is the right goal, the bull's eye of the target. He is grace, mercy, forgiveness, and Love. But how do people come to know the grace, mercy, forgiveness, and Love of God? By going through a learning process to gain a knowledge of good and evil. Humans needed the tree in order to grow mentally and spiritually. The tree taught us to understand God's goodness and Love. God's purpose in all this was for humans to learn and admit that we are not God, and for humans to allow Him to be God, the Supreme Creator.

> *"Never soul was set free without being made to feel its slavery."*
>
> George MacDonald,
> writer, England[2]

The Story of the Human Race

The story of Adam and Eve teaches us several things. First, it reminds us of how we all came to know good and evil. It is the story of the entire human race. Each time we sin, we come to know good and evil as God knows it. But we don't become the God that He is. Instead, our sin distances us from God, and we realize how often we listen to the serpent. Yet that distance stirs us to turn and see Him beckoning for us to come to Him.

The second thing the story of Adam and Eve tells us is that how we perceive God defines our relationship with God. If we see God as warm and loving, we feel that our relationship with Him is warm and loving. If we see God as cold and rejecting, we feel that our relationship with Him is cold and rejecting. If we think God is just for polite philosophical conversations, that's the way we see our relationship with Him. It all depends on the "glasses" we look through.

> *The good people taste your goodness,*
> *The whole people taste your health,*
> *The true people taste your truth,*
> *The bad ones can't figure you out.*
>
> *Psalm 18:25, 26,*
> *The Message*

Third, the story of Adam and Eve shows us that if we choose God, we choose a relationship of grace, forgiveness, and Love. If we reject God, all that's left is cause and effect (karma, law). Then it's easy to accuse God of being angry (or "full of wrath," as the Bible sometimes puts it), damning us because of our bad karma.

All humans look at God through guilt-colored glasses, because all humans fail to live up to the Standard. So when our sins are not too bad, we see God as simply angry. But when our sins are terrible, we view God as a tyrant, and we can hardly even think of Him as a personal God. In reality, God is not a tyrant. Even His anger is simply a sense of displeasure, while human anger is associated with pride, vengeance, and bitterness. So we can't speak about God's anger in the same way that we say we have anger. It's true that ancient people spoke of the "wrath and anger" of God. All the Old Testament talks that way. But that was because they were viewing God through karma and its guilt-colored glasses.

If people view God as being angry because they don't do good, then the next step in the head-thing is to decide we can get God to stop being angry if we'll just do good. Which, of course, we quickly realize we can't do. Still, most of us in the world try our best. But even our best isn't good enough to live up to the Standard of Perfect Love. It's like a barista at Portland Brew handing you a half cup of latte. "Hey," you say. "I ordered a whole cup. You didn't fill it full." The latte just doesn't measure up to the standard. It's not *filled full*. It's not *full-filled*. Or as we most often hear in terms of law: It's not fulfilled. We are constantly trying to hand God a cup that's half full. And it's the best we can do under karma. Humans can't fulfill the moral law, because what we see as law is based on the Standard of Perfect Love, and only God is Perfect Love

> *"All my life I have been seeking to climb out of the pit of my besetting sins and I cannot do it and I never will unless a hand is let down to draw me up."*
>
> — *Seneca, Roman statesman*
> *during the time of the New Testament writers*[3]

The ironic thing is that God's image in us, the Standard of Love, our natural moral law, is supposed to bring a beautiful, deep, full life (peace, kindness, goodness, beauty, etc. into eternity). Instead, because we violate that Standard, it brings death (hatred, fear, distortion, depression, etc.). But our inability to keep good karma has not taken God by surprise. And He's not stressed out over what to do about it, as we'll see in the next chapter.

Where we are so far. . .

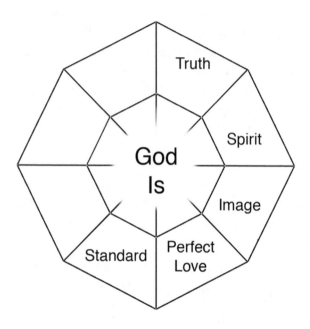

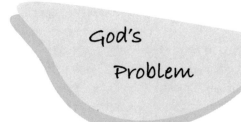

Chapter 8

God's
Problem

All people bear identically an image they can't attain,
a Standard they can't live up to,
a law they can't keep,
a Love they can't achieve.

Because the knowledge of good and evil exists within us, we know to "do good, do good, do good." But we can't. That's a problem. And God knew we would have that problem. Like the student in the first chapter, we might ask here, "What is God doing? Playing a game?"

This Impossible Bull's Eye

From the beginning, God knew that humans could not actually do what He had created them to do. So whatever happens in this world is ultimately God's problem. After all, He's the Creator. He placed the knowledge of goodness, the law of nature within us. So it's God who made the Standard too hard to live up to. He's the One who made the law too hard to keep.

(Of course that's like a person who doesn't know how to swim saying, "It's the pool's fault. I can't get across the pool, because it's got water in it." A pool full of water is the standard, the measurement of whether a person can swim or not. So the imperfection isn't with the pool. It's with the person who can't swim.)

That's the way it is with us and God. The imperfection isn't with God. He *is* the Standard. He *is* the Perfect Love. He *is* the image replicated in us. He doesn't have to do anything but *exist*, and next to Him we are fully aware of how we miss the target. The imperfection is with us. Still, God must do something about this impossible bull's eye, or we'll dig ourselves deeper and deeper into the consequences of bad karma. Which ends up being hatred and death and complete separation from the One who created us in the first place. We don't want that. And neither does God. He didn't create us just to condemn us. He didn't create us just to watch us try and try and ultimately fail.

So God took responsibility when He created us. His plan was for humans not only to have the knowledge of good and evil, but also to share His life. He knew that humans could not love as He did and that eventually He Himself would have to release them from the cycle of cause and effect that brings condemnation and death.

> "I thirst for Thee, O God; when shall I meet Thee? Is there a friend, a saint, a God's-Own who'll take me to the Lord? Without Him I'm comforted not."
> — from the <u>Granth</u>, sacred book of the Sikhs[1]

Dia-Logos

Let's do a little head-gut thing here with dialogue. We'll go logically through some questions, and you answer honestly by what your gut tells you.

- Did you create the world?

- How can you be sure? (I'm assuming you're just human, not God.)

• Can you be as perfectly loving and good as God is?

• Why can you not love perfectly as God loves?
  Ah. So the creation can never be the Creator.

• Does the cause and effect principle of karma (law) have to
  be fulfilled? (Remember the laws of nature: gravity, light,
  chemistry — predictable effect always follows a cause.
  This gives the world order, not chaos. It's the same with
  karma: good cause, good effect; bad cause, bad effect.)

• We know that if we'll just love perfectly, we can keep the
  whole law. Is the law (karma) for people to keep or for
  God to keep?

• Is the Standard, the law of Love (be kind, have mercy, forgive, be honest, etc.), meant to bring life or death?

• If it's meant to bring life, why does it condemn instead?
  Because people can't fulfill the law, and law is non-personal. It can't forgive. Is that what your gut tells you?

• If you do good, do you deserve to get something good in
  return? And if you do bad, do you deserve to get something bad in return?

• Is there any escape from that law of karma?

• If humans can't keep the law, who can?

God is the only one who can keep the law, to live up to the Standard, which is Him. Yet the law, the Standard, exists so that humans can have a beautiful, deep, full life.

> So if the law is going to be kept perfectly,
> God must become human,
> Born under karma (the law),
> To do for humans
> What humans cannot do for themselves
> So that humans, destined to death,
> Can instead find true Life.

The Hero

Most popular movies and books tell about a hero. The hero saves the world from the diabolical scientist who is threatening to destroy it. Or the hero saves someone on the battlefield in war. Or the hero saves the home of a family who is going to be kicked out by the developers of a mall. Or the hero slays the evil dragon that's ravaging the countryside. Whatever the story hero does, he or she shows love, courage, and justice.

These kinds of stories and myths may be fictional, but they contain a truth that is rooted in what we know we know: We need someone who is loving, courageous, and just to save us. To release us from the damning power of sin, God Himself had to become our Divine Hero. He had to keep the law for us and slay the power of sin and the sting of death.

God, as Jesus, was the Divine Hero who became a human to do the work of *life*. He knew good and evil, but He always chose the good. So He kept good karma all his life. As God-man, He successfully kept the law's demands for us, lived up to the Standard for us, attained God's image for us, Loved perfectly for us.

"He was made what we are that He might make us what He is Himself."
—Saint Irenaeus[2]

He also became a human to do the work of *death*. He took the condemnation of bad karma for us. Though the actions in His life were good, He accepted the law's requirements for justice and received the negative consequence of *our* bad karma, willingly dying a convicted criminal's death for us. But just as we have choice, so Jesus had a choice: to back off or to stand firm. He stood firm, loving and respecting everyone equally: rich and poor, educated and uneducated, male and female, Jew and Gentile. Some people hated Him for that. And God allowed their karma to play itself out in arresting, convicting, and crucifying Him. For the first time, cause and effect did not match. The law of karma was turned on its head. Perfect Love received the consequence deserved by bad karma. As a result, bad karma can now receive the consequence of Perfect Love.

> *"God is generous. The cross is the sign of addition."*
> -- George Sweeting, pastor and writer[3]

Still, it was not Jesus' death that completed the work. It was Jesus' resurrection from death that settled the victory over sin. His physical resurrection showed that God's grace applied to death in *our* bodies too. When Jesus came back to life, we got the hope of life beyond death for ourselves as well. Not just a never-ending life, but an *eternal life*. With God.

Eternal Life is not just living forever after we die, although that's part of it. Jesus said, "Eternal life is this: that people be constantly knowing you, the only genuine God and Jesus Christ whom You sent."[4] The Greek word used for "knowing" in this sentence means a knowledge that comes by experience, not by intellectual facts. Eternal Life is a quality of life that we can experience now (and forever) in relationship with the One Who is Perfect Love.[5]

The Bridge

We saw earlier that all philosophies and religions have had some concept of a bridge or mediator to bring harmony between themselves and their concepts of the One we call God: YHWH (Yahweh) of the Jews, the Supreme Brahman of the Hindus, Nirvana of the Buddhists, the Unnamed of the Taoists, Allah of Islam. However, for all philosophies and religions, the concept of a *bridge* to God has been Law. Even many Christians think that acceptance by God depends on how well they obey the instructions they read as rules in the Bible. That's law. Karma.

But God never meant for law to be the mediator, and He never said our relationship with Him was based on keeping the law. He always intended for His *Love* to be the mediator. Besides, God is willing and able to do everything that the Standard of Perfect Love requires of us humans. So He bridged the gap. The God-man fulfilled the law, lived up to the Standard, kept perfect karma for humanity, including self-sacrifice, the ultimate act of Love. He was the mediator. In effect, God says to us, "Do you want to trade? I'll give you my Life of Perfect Love, if you'll give me your life of wanting Me. All you have to do is accept my death as the consequence of your bad karma." There it is: the offer of peace and harmony with the Creator.

Each person, then, is free to accept or reject that offer, because God has given each human being free will. We are all free to make our own choices and experience the effects of our own karma. So if we don't want God to fulfill the law for us, or if we don't believe He really did, then we are left with nothing but karma, law's power over us, for cause and effect will continue to operate on us. But if we accept God's taking the conse-quence of our bad karma, then we are set free from the condemnation of law, because the cause and effect of karma applies to Jesus' life and death instead of ours.

Answer of Answers

I'm the Answer of answers,
Peace of all peace.
Rest in my shade,
Be at ease.
For I myself
Am the Lord your God
And I have taken up your cause.
I have taken up your cause.

Hurting hearts are mine to heal.
I feel all the hurts you feel.
For you I shouldered all the blame.
That is why I came.
That is why I came.

Karma (law) can't be the mediator, because it is impersonal. It can't forgive. All it can do is judge and condemn us when we don't love perfectly. But God is personal. He *can* forgive. So as Jesus, God did what karma could never do: He became the mediator. He bridged the gap.

> "The hand of GOD has turned the tide!
> The hand of GOD is raised in victory!
> The hand of GOD has turned the tide!"
> — Psalm 118:16, <u>The Message</u>

The best man can give is law:
>   Moses introduced law.
>   Buddha was enlightened to law.
>   Greek philosophers described law.
>   Lao Tze identified law in nature.
>   Mohammed set up law.
>   Only God Himself could forgive the violation of law.
>   By Jesus' Perfect Love,
>   He did.

Chapter 9

In the Skin

Some people believe in reincarnation. But almost all people believe in **incarnation**. *Caro* means "flesh" in Latin. So incarnation means "in the flesh." In the skin. (Okay, bones and blood and muscles and tendons, too.) But how can we say that everyone believes in incarnation? Because everyone is incarnated. Everyone knows they exist. In a body. Our bodies house the real us, our thoughts, ideas, feelings, spirits. If you hear a song you like, it may incarnate in you, and you find your mind singing it over and over again without your permission. It's worse if it happens with a song you don't like. Anyway, the simple idea that we are incarnated, meaning we exist within a body, is pretty much a no-brainer.

What we've seen over the last few chapters is that being created in the image of God means that God incarnated His image in us, the Standard of goodness and Love. We view it as moral law; still, it's incarnated within us, this knowledge of right and wrong.

The incarnation that's hard for some people to accept is the incarnation of God Himself. (Which is kind of strange. If *we* can be incarnate, why could God *not be*?) You believe that you are incarnated. But why do you believe that God incarnated Himself as Jesus? Even though the last chapter ran through some of this, it went by kind of fast. Let's spend a little while longer on this, because it's where a lot of people take a detour. We won't go back into history and try to prove that Jesus lived as God-man and walked the earth. It's okay to do that, and there are some good books about that. But there's a gut-level way to look at it, because it's Truth that you can *know* you know.

Let's Start With Love

Gut-level, people know that Love is a good thing. We're not talking sex. (Sorry.) Sex can be an expression of love, but sex can also be totally without love. It can be an act of undisciplined lust or even hatred. The love we're talking about is kind, compassionate, and respectful. Yet it's even more than that. Because while love is respectful, respect doesn't necessarily mean love. A person can be kind, respectful, and tolerant for selfish reasons, hoping to become popular or to get good grades or to get a date with someone.

So when we talk about Love, we're talking about *all* the characteristics of love, everything that would live up to the Standard, the image of God within us. It's the Love that we know would obey every natural moral law, the Love that is good karma. What do we know we know about this kind of love?

1. Love comes from a pure heart.
   Love never gives up.
   Love cares more for others than for self.
   Love doesn't want what it doesn't have.
   Love doesn't strut,
   Doesn't have a swelled head,
   Doesn't force itself on others,
   Isn't always "me first,"
   Doesn't fly off the handle,
   Doesn't keep score of the sins of others,

Doesn't revel when others grovel,
Takes pleasure in the flowering of truth,
Puts up with anything,
Trusts God always,
Always looks for the best,
Never looks back,
But keeps going to the end.
Love never dies.

— 1 Corinthians 13:4-8, <u>The Message</u>

If someone loves like the above list describes, most people would say that person is loving. That's something we know we know. The descriptions in that list are all qualities of eternity. There would be a beautiful, deep, full life in a world where love and only love reigned supreme. Humans really want this kind of love more than anything, but human action can't achieve it. We know that if this kind of love is ever to exist in a human being, it has to happen by God incarnating Himself.

2. Love forgives.

In ancient times, the whole world saw pain and suffering as the effect of previous evil actions, the law of karma. So when Jesus' disciples saw a man who had been born blind, they asked, "Who sinned: this man or his parents?" They thought his blindness was the result of someone's bad karma. When Jesus healed the blind man, it was equivalent to saying that the man's sins had been forgiven, his bad karma erased. This amazed the people.

Another time, some men carried their paralyzed friend to Jesus. Jesus did not say, "Pick up your bed and walk." Instead, he said, "Your sins are forgiven." This was new. Never before had anyone come forgiving sins.

The leaders were offended. "Who do you think you are?" they asked. "Only God can forgive sins."

Jesus said, "Which is easier to say: 'Your sins are forgiven,' or 'Take up your bed and walk'?" Jesus was pointing out that they were wrong to believe that sins couldn't be forgiven, that bad karma would have to be reaped for generations.

But that's what all of Asian philosophy believes, even today. Karma 'R Us: We are our karma; we came from our karma; we will be our karma. Every evil action must have its effect upon the person's future. That would be right if no one could keep the law. But what if God came into the world as a human? Surely He would live and act as God. Since love is humble and unselfish, He would be humble and unselfish. He would obey the natural moral law by loving perfectly.

You see, the law, the Standard, can be fulfilled only by a human. Because the law is for humans, not for God. As we've said before, God *is* the Standard (what humans see as the natural moral law). So He lives up to it — no problem. It's humans who have trouble with it. And it's humans who must achieve it. So the law can be fulfilled only by a human loving perfectly.

But only God can love perfectly.

So the law can be fulfilled only by God becoming human.

God, as Perfect Love, would have to do what the whole world believed could not be done: forgive sins, trump karma.

3. Love is active and creative.

Two of the greatest facts we know are:

(1) At the very center of our beings is life.
(2) At the very center of ultimate happiness is pure love.

Love's nature is to give life. It must express itself; it must interact. For example, if a guy loves a girl, he is consumed with the desire to have her see and feel and receive his love. So Love always looks for different ways to communicate itself.

God's love never changes, yet it's constantly new and creative.

It's eternal and faithful.

It extends its beauty in creation.

It expresses itself to humanity.

It recreates itself in us.

Divine Love keeps the whole material world moving; it is the creative energy that scientists seek to discover and define. It acts as the highest expression of unselfishness. So, if God became one of us, wouldn't He:

receive the children,

reach to outsiders,

touch the lepers, heal the sick,

raise the dead,

and explain His ways:

"Come to me, you who are weary."

"God loves the world."

"The only way you can know God's reign in your life is to realize your need for Him. . .The way to see God is to be pure in heart. . ."[1]

We know, gut-level, that if and when God came, He would *have* to express His love in these ways.

> "You should point to the whole man Jesus and say, 'That is God.'" — Martin Luther[2]

4. Love's highest expression is self-sacrifice.

Everyone knows this. You don't have to prove it. Earlier, we saw how movies, stories, myths, and legends have self-sacrificing heroes. Mystery writer James N. Frey says, "The mystery hero is self-sacrificing; that is the key to the hero/detective's character."[3] Think again about Ghandi, Mother Theresa, and the rescue workers of 9/11. They sacrificed their lives for others. Everyone knows that the supreme act of love is to give up your life for someone else. So if God came to earth as a human, then we know, gut-level, that He would show Love in its highest form: self-sacrifice. And, of course, the cross of Christ demonstrates this exact pinnacle of Love.

> *"Alexander, Caesar, Charlemagne, and myself founded empires; but on what foundation did we rest the creations of our genius? Upon force. Jesus Christ founded an empire upon love; and at this hour millions of men would die for Him."*
> — Napoleon Bonaparte, emperor of France, early 1800's[4]

Love vs. Karma

You'll remember that we talked about how we experience God's incarnated image, His Standard of Love within us, as a law we must keep (do good, be kind, be honest, etc.). But we also experience His image of Love within us as our own desire to express truth, beauty, and justice, qualities that almost everyone in the world values.

We humans keep reaching for the greatest and highest. We want the perfect figure or physique, the perfect complexion. Athletes want to have greater strength, run farther and faster, throw the perfect curve ball, set a world record. Musicians, actors, dancers, painters, and writers practice hours on end, hoping to perfect their skills. We want the perfect job, the perfect relationship. We are not satisfied to leave things the way they are. We want to move onward and upward. We want to excel.

That's because God is perfect beauty, perfect creativity, perfect strength, perfect wisdom. He is the Standard, and gut-level we all want to be like Him.

Have you ever lain down at night feeling very satisfied in your spirit, because you did something that day that was beautiful or truthful or loving? Why do you feel so good about it? Because you have lived up to the image of God, the Standard within you. You have fulfilled the moral law.

Of course, the next night, you may go to bed curled in a fetal position, because you feel so ashamed of how rudely you spoke to your mom and dad or how insensitive you were to your best friend. We all know we don't perfectly live the Love of God incarnated in us by His image. Even if we could reincarnate through six million lifetimes, we'd never live up to God's image of Perfect Love.

Only God can live up to His own image. So it is an absolute necessity for God to do what humans can't: live up to His image in us by keeping the law for us. He *had* to come in the flesh. He *had* to fulfill His own human requirements.

> "There is no pillow so soft as a clear conscience."
> — French proverb[5]

Back to love: By loving perfectly, a person would be keeping the law perfectly (good karma). And anyone who can keep the law perfectly will be in total control of himself. He will have won over the law. Law will no longer be in charge of him; instead, he will be the one who has authority over law. Love rules over law by fulfilling its demands, its requirements.

Have you ever played Spades? If you have, you know that a playing card with a spade on it "trumps" or wins over any card with a heart or diamond or club on it. And the Ace of Spades trumps everything. (You may have played other trump

> "But there is only one thing that has power completely, and that is love. Because when a man loves, he seeks no power, and therefore he has power."
> — Alan Paton, <u>Cry, the Beloved Country</u>[6]

games in which a different suit of cards is the trump. The principle is the same.) Well, God's Love expressed in Jesus' self-sacrifice trumps law. It takes control of law. God's Love wins over law. In other words: **Love trumps karma**.

<u>I Have Killed</u>

I have killed death.
I have ruined ruin.
I have depleted depletion.
I have destroyed destruction.
I am God.
The Builder.
The Encourager.
The Creator.
On the embers of the old,
I build the new.
Out of the depths of destruction,
I bring forth life.
I do restore what the locusts have eaten.
    In fuller measure.
    In greater breadth.
Because I am God.
Because I am Love.

God's Love and forgiveness do not do away with natural moral law. But they do become the elements by which law is fulfilled or completed. Human karma (works, actions) can never live up to any law: not the dhamma, not the conditioned Brahman, not the Tao, not the Torah, not the Qur'an, or any other law. But the Perfect Love of Jesus *can* live up to law, because it's greater than law. Love trumps karma. So now, though law is the Standard, it's love that's in control of anybody who accepts the One who is Perfect Love.

Jesus is the One who completes:

-everything the Buddhists hope the dhamma will do for them,

-everything the Hindus hope the conditioned Brahman will do for them,

-everything the Taoists hope the Tao will do for them,

-everything the Jews hope the Torah will do for them,

-everything the Muslims hope the Qur'an will do for them,

-everything Christian legalists hope that obeying rules will do for them.

> *And some who have heard it don't understand that God didn't come to condemn the world.*

Jesus died once and for all. So everyone is forgiven. It's just that not everyone knows it or accepts it yet. And some who have heard it don't understand that God didn't come to condemn the world. The world was condemned already because of bad karma. God came to save the world from the consequences of bad karma. That's all. No, let me rephrase it: that's ALL. Everyone. Totally. Completely. Entirely. Cosmically. Universally. ALL.

God rescued us from dead-end alleys and dark dungeons. He's set us up in the kingdom of the Son he loves so much, the Son who got us out of the pit we were in, got rid of the sins we were doomed to keep repeating.

We look at this Son and see the God who cannot be seen. We look at this Son and see God's original purpose in everything created. For everything, absolutely everything, above and below, visible and invisible, rank after rank after rank of angels — everything got started in him and finds its purpose in him. He was there before any of it came into existence and holds it all together right up to this moment. . .

He was supreme in the beginning and — leading the resurrection parade — he is supreme in the end. From beginning to end he's there, towering far above everything, everyone. So spacious is he, so roomy, that everything of God finds its proper place in him without crowding. Not only that, but all the broken and dislocated pieces of the universe — people and things, animals and atoms — get properly fixed and fit together in vibrant harmonies, all because of his death, his blood that poured down from the Cross.

— Colossians 1:13-20, The Message

To recap the news of the hour: We know that we our-selves are incarnated, because God has put life and love and personality into our bodies. So it should not seem strange to think that God could incarnate Himself. It makes sense to think that God could become human for the purpose of doing for humans what we can't do for ourselves: keep the natural moral law. Only God can keep the law perfectly. So if the law is ever going to be kept perfectly, if karma is ever going to be com-pletely good, God *must* become human. Which He did.

The Holy Child
He is the Ancient Wisdom of the World,
The Word Creative, Beautiful and True,
The Nameless of Innumerable Names,
Ageless forever, yet Forever New.

- Charles Carroll Albertson, writer 1865 [7]

Where we are so far. . .

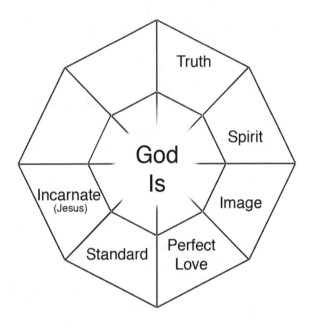

Chapter 10

New Age,
Old Stuff

Spirituality is the deepest thing we humans think about. Sure, we get busy with whatever-we-need-to-do, whenever-we-need-to-do-it. But the spiritual is never far from us, because of course, we are made in God's image. Spirituality is popular right now, and that's good, because it means you and your friends are thinking about God and seeking God. And enjoying it! (It wasn't always that way.)

All of this means we hear and read lots of things about Zen/Buddhism, Tao, and New Age. Good things. Because as we've seen, these religions focus on kindness and goodness, beauty and love. And there's certainly nothing wrong with kindness, goodness, beauty, and love. God knows our world needs all the kindness, goodness, beauty, and love we can get. After all, those qualities were His idea. In fact, those qualities are who He is. So let's explore Zen/ Buddhism and New Age spirituality.

But first, let's agree on something. If you're reading this, and you're already condemning Zen/Buddhism, Tao, and New Age spirituality, then STOP! I mean stop condemning, not reading. Just take a deep breath and remember that God did not send His Son into the world to condemn the world.[1] If Jesus doesn't condemn, we can't either. A lot of Christians turn to Zen/Buddhism or Tao or New Age, because they feel accepted and loved by people who embrace those philosophies, and they feel condemned and judged by Christians. . .who are supposed to be the most loving people in the world. Go figure. When we judge and condemn people, we put ourselves in a "we're in - you're out" frame of mind, which is essentially called pride. And the karma of pride is "you boast, you fall."[2] You don't want to go there.

> ... they feel condemned and judged by Christians. . . who are supposed to be the most loving people in the world. Go figure.

Okay, so with love and a humble gut, let's look at the world around us, which includes our family and friends. The first thing to know is that New Age is Old Stuff. In the U.S., it started back in the 1960's when the Beatles and other groups were popular. Many of these celebrities liked to visit their gurus in India and Asia, and the thought-for-the-decade was *PEACE* with its symbol of two fingers raised (like V for Victory, only meaning Victory through Peace). Well, considering Jesus is the Prince of Peace, that's not such a bad thing to go for. In fact, Jesus got real popular back then too.

But New Age is even older than that. New Age is simply a Westernized Hinduism with some Buddhism thrown in. (Zen is a form of Buddhism.) And of course, Hinduism and Buddhism were around long before Jesus was born. So New Age is ancient, even though it is packaged as something fresh and new in our culture.

The Divine Source

Part of the new look and sound of the New Age has to do with changing the words "Unknowable" or "Unreachable

Brahman" to the English word "God." So people who have grown up in a culture like ours (based on Judaism and Christianity) tend to project their own concepts of God on the New Age word *God*. We might think they're saying something we already believe. But they're not. When they talk about God, they mean Something *non-personal*.

New Age philosophy calls God a Divine Source or Essence or Energy. In a word: "It." But they say that "It" is somehow real and knowable. This is an example of the kinds of contradictions you will hear in this philosophy if you listen carefully. In their minds, "all" springs from the Energy which fills "all." They stress that by plugging into the Energy Source, people can experience healing and miracles. But they say that this Essence or Energy's source is found within each person. Which sounds right, probably because it's exactly backward. In reality, each person's source is found in the Essence or Energy, who is a personal being, the God of Perfect Love, whose image is within each person.

Watch out for people who are signaling a left turn, but are turning right.

One problem with an impersonal "It" is that you can't love an "It." And an "It" can't love you. People don't love Brahman or Allah or the Unnamed or the dhamma. These "unreachables" are not personal.

The Perfect Love we humans crave is nonexistent if God is impersonal. On the other hand, the God who created us in His image is constantly
  revealing Himself to us,
    communicating with us,
      expressing His love and beauty to us,
        inviting us to come closer to Him and
          know Him better,
            telling us He knows us better than we know
              ourselves.
                That's personal. And that's Love.

New Age philosophy and Zen/Buddhism and every other religion are part of what is called pluralism. Pluralism — think *plural* — means "many viewpoints." America was once considered to be a Christian nation. But it is now a pluralistic nation, which means that the overall viewpoint of our society is that you can worship Jesus Christ as God, or the Buddha as God, or anything else as God. Or not. God can be personal to you, or non-personal. You can call God "It" or Brahman or Nirvana or Allah or Essence or Energy Source. It makes no difference in pluralism, for what pluralism considers to be divine is simply love expressed as a community living together in justice, peace, forgiveness, kindness, tolerance, and non-judgmentalness.

Yet a loving community is important, isn't it? Doesn't God want us to live together in justice and peace, forgiveness, kindness, tolerance, and non-judgmentalness? True. That's what gives pluralism its strength. That's why it looks so good. It asks all people to receive each other in tolerance and respect, to be good and kind to others. It says that all religions teach universal truths: speak honestly, be kind, be merciful, and so forth. That's true too. All people, gut-level, believe that this is the common Standard. It's the law of karma.

"You can't drive straight on a twisting lane."
--Russian proverb [3]

But there's a major problem with pluralism: If God can be whatever or whoever you believe, then your belief is simply an opinion that's just as good as any other person's opinion. So you are creating your own standard, your own sense of right and wrong. And each person always brings biases, moral weaknesses, and hidden agendas into their opinion of what's right and what's wrong. What one person decides is right may be different from what another person decides. That makes it impossible to get the unity of lifestyle that pluralists want. Only God's Love shown through Jesus can bring about true unity.

This brings us to another problem with pluralism. It's all *for* the concept of love and the idea of knowing God, but it's against the deity of Jesus. That's because if Jesus is Divine, then God is personal and intimate, and we feel accountable to Him for the choices we make. If Jesus is Divine, and God is personal, then we can't create our own standard, our own sense of right and wrong. But if Jesus is not Divine, then He is simply a teacher equal to Buddha, Lao Tze, Mohammed, or the Hindu philosophers, which means we can say God is impersonal. Then it's easier *not* to feel accountable. We can create our own standard and do whatever we want. We can't offend an impersonal God, because it has no heart to offend.

But by now, you know the problem an impersonal God causes: Karma is still karma. Law is still law. People are still people and can't keep the law. We all have bad karma and will have to harvest what we plant. If God is not personal, there is no one to forgive or grant mercy. That, of course, is why Hindus and Buddhists believe in reincarnation and rebirth of karma. Cycles of rebirths into other life forms allow us to get the bad consequences we deserve for the bad karma we do now. And we keep being reincarnated until we work out all our bad karma. But New Age teachers don't talk too much about their belief in reincarnation. Gut-level, it's not so easy for us to believe in reincarnation. The New Age focus on freedom and goodness is more popular. Because gut-level, we all know that freedom and goodness are right.

So Jesus is truly the speed bump for pluralism and New Age. These philosophies want to get over Him, past Him, around Him as fast as they can. But while people who accept these philosophies avoid Jesus, they are very willing to talk about christ.

christ and Christ

On his way home to the U.S. from Asia, my friend Ken had a three-hour layover at an airport in California. In the waiting area, he happened to sit next to a young man who had a laptop computer. Having been in Asia for several years, Ken had not seen many laptops, so he asked the man about it. As they talked, the young man told Ken that his father was a leader of the New Age movement in Dallas, Texas. So the conversation turned to religion. The young man said, "Christ is in every person."

Now when we Christians hear the word *christ*, we think of Jesus. But that's not what this young man was saying. He was saying that he believed that the image of God was in every person. That, we can agree with. But the young man did not mean that Jesus is the Christ. Instead, what he was talking about is often called "christ-consciousness."

Let's take a look at this word "christ." It's the Greek word "christos" used in the New Testament to mean

"the anointed one,"
the one chosen,
or the one declared to be sacred,
devoted to the worship of God.

"Christos" is the same as the Old Testament Hebrew word "messiah." Before Jesus came, "messiah" and "christ" were common nouns, not proper nouns. They were generic words. In the Old Testament, you can find "messiah" used to refer to kings and priests chosen by God or devoted to the worship of God. Psalm 105:15 refers to prophets as *hoi christou Theou*, "the christ of God" or "the anointed of God." Even Cyrus, a king of Persia and Babylon, is called God's anointed, "messiah," translated "christ" in Greek.

So the definition of "christ" has not always been Jesus. And the Jews were not the only people who looked for some kind of messiah to come. Even before Jesus came, many cultures looked for a chosen one. The Karen (Kah-rin') tribes of Burma and northern Thailand and the Lahu (Lah'-hoo) of southeast Asia and southern China had legends of the coming of the "man in white," or "the man with the white book," or "the man on a white horse coming as a redeemer for their peoples."[4]

Why do the different cultures feel the need for a bridge, a mediator? Because they know they do not live up to the Standard within them. They do not have perfect karma. And they know they cannot find mercy and forgiveness by themselves. They want a mediator to take their out-of-sync lives and put them in-sync with the Divine. This awareness of the need for a bridge or mediator is "christ-consciousness." We've already seen how the Greeks' concept of a mediator was the *Logos* or *Word*. The same "christ-consciousness" exists in Buddhism with the dhamma, in Hinduism with the conditioned Brahman, in Taoism with the Tao, in Judaism with the Torah (although they would not call it christ-consciousness). So you can agree with someone who tells you they believe christ is in every person. In the sense of the generic christ or christ-consciousness, they are right.

But the followers of each philosophy or religion try to live up to the rules of their particular mediator so that they will have good karma. They hope that someday they will be good enough to come into harmony with their idea of the Divine Essence. Of course, we know that no human being can live up to the Standard; no one has perfectly good karma. So no one can cross any of these "bridges."

None of these philosophies or religions ever dreamed

that the Divine Essence would build a bridge to them. But that's just what happened with God incarnate as Jesus. He came as "the anointed one," the one chosen or declared to be sacred, devoted to the worship of God. Jesus the God-man turned the generic, common noun *christ* into the proper noun, the name *Christ*. He turned a consciousness into flesh-and-blood reality. He became a living, breathing mediator.

If people reject Jesus as the Christ, the bridge, the Way, then all that's left is for them to live up to the moral law on their own. They can call it dhamma or Tao or conditioned Brahman or Torah. But each of these puts the burden of perfection on human shoulders. Each of these requires people to have perfect karma. Which no one has ever had. And no one ever will. With law as a mediator, everyone stands condemned.

But God took the burden of perfection upon Himself:

Jesus is **the image of God**[5]

Jesus lived a life of **Perfect Love**.

Jesus lived up to the **Standard**.

Jesus kept (fulfilled) **the moral law** (karma).

Jesus is the **Christ**, the mediator, the bridge, the One chosen to be the Way.

Jesus fulfills all these concepts of the essence of Truth. Christ is completely real and abundantly alive through the God-man.

> We got the basics from Moses,
> and then this exuberant giving and receiving,
> This endless knowing and understanding —
> all this came through Jesus, the Messiah.
> No one has ever seen God,
> not so much as a glimpse.
> This one-of-a-kind God-Expression,
> who exists at the very heart of the Father,
> has made him plain as day.
> — John 1:16-18, <u>The Message</u>

As Christians, we know that Jesus is the Christ within us. But christ (christ-consciousness, the need for a mediator) was not put there by our believing in Jesus. Instead, the christ-consciousness within us came to life and became Christ only when we realized that Jesus is the Christ, the "in the skin" fulfillment of the generic christ-consciousness. He *is* the mediator.

Jesus asked his friends one day, "Who do people say I am?"

"Some say you're John the Baptist," said his friends. "Others say you're Elijah or Jeremiah, or one of the other prophets."

Peter was listening to all this when he had an "aha! moment." He began to absorb the earth-shaking importance of the Truth that was burning in his gut. I can imagine that his eyes grew wide with the awe of it. "*You!*" he said. "**You** are Christ! *You* are the Son of the living God!"

And I can imagine that Jesus laughed, sharing the pleasure of Peter's discovery. "You heard from my Father in heaven!" said Jesus.[6]

Peter saw that Jesus was not just *a* messiah, *a* christ, but *the* Messiah, *the* Christ sent from God. And how did Peter know? He had a sudden, gut-level understanding that this Jesus who stood before him was the Anointed One. The Spirit of God confirmed Truth to Peter's spirit, and he knew that he knew.

Where we are so far. . .

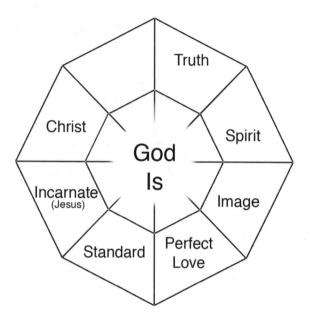

* * * * * *

A Byte of World Philosophies & Religions

If God hadn't written His image, the Standard, on our hearts, there would be much greater variety in philosophies. Instead, all the religions and philosophies we've looked at have the same basic problem: They try to approach God through law.

Philosophy or Religion	Main Belief
Ancient Greeks and Romans	God is not personal. Many gods (polytheism).
Hinduism	God is not personal. All is God (pantheism).
Buddhism and Atheism	There is no God.
Taoism	God is not personal.
Islam and Judaism	God is personal, but He is our God, not yours.

The main problem with these philosophies is:

- Hinduism's Brahman cannot forgive or extend mercy for karma (the law of cause and effect).
- Buddhism's dhamma cannot forgive or extend mercy for karma.
- Atheism cannot find forgiveness or mercy for karma.
- Taoism's "Unnamed" cannot forgive or extend mercy for karma.
- Allah of Islam gives law that is wrathful and cannot forgive or bring mercy for karma.
- Judaism has a law (karma) no one can keep.

No human can live up to the Standard, the natural law, karma. Only Perfect Love can achieve the Standard, fulfill the law, have perfectly good karma.

The only way for a human to achieve Perfect Love is to get it as a gift from Love Himself.

Chapter 11

The

Three-Letter

"S" Word

(Sorry. This is the other three-letter "S" Word.
The one nobody wants to talk about.)

Have you ever taken archery, or seen someone shooting an arrow at a target? Or maybe you've played darts and aimed at a target hanging on a wall. If you have, you know that the bull's eye in the center of the target is not so easy to hit. But it's the mark you're aiming for.

The word *sin* in Greek means "missing the mark." The mark is the Standard that's in us because of God's image in us. As we know, that Standard is Perfect Love, which we see as the "do good, do good, do good" of natural moral law. So to sin means to fail to be as loving and good as our Creator. It's missing the mark, not living up to the Standard of Love.

Parents are usually the ones who have the responsibility of teaching their progeny to "do good, do good, do good." Teachers have this responsibility too. Of course, parents and teachers can't do good perfectly themselves. And they know we can't either, but they hold up a certain standard they expect us to achieve. Sometimes it seems like the standard is perfection.

Like most parents, yours probably told you to make your bed. And they probably told you it's wrong not to pick up after yourself. But are these things really wrong? Are they sin? Can something be wrong that is not a sin? Is God going to damn you because you ran inside the house, or because you were being careless at dinnertime and knocked your drink over? Sometimes parents and teachers react to stuff as though we've committed the crime of the century. (Could overreaction be a sin?)

Parents and teachers usually don't think about making any distinction between different categories of wrong actions or bad karma. So we grow up with a broad notion of right and wrong and sin. Take making your bed or keeping your room clean, for example. Your gut probably tells you that it's not the best thing in the world to leave your bed unmade, but it's not a sin. Maybe that's why it irritates us to be treated by parents and teachers as though we're sinning when we've figured out that it may not really matter if we leave our room messy. (At least it doesn't matter from one perspective.) But before we go proclaiming victory for the messy room, let's look at the categories of right and wrong.

Social Convention

First there is social convention. Manners. Or what we would call "being polite." These rights and wrongs may change according to what culture you're in. For example, in many Asian cultures, it's right to remove your shoes just before or after you enter a house. But that's not important to most Americans (unless they are of Asian background or have adopted this custom). So right and wrong in the area of social convention can be a family or cultural standard, but not the Standard that *everyone* knows gut-level is right and wrong.

Social convention can also change generationally. For example, fifty years ago, everyone used the words "stewardess," "actress," "postman and postmistress." But now those labels are considered wrong. We say "flight attendant" and "postal worker." And every theatre performer is now an "actor." So another way of talking about this category of right and wrong is to say it's "correct vs. incorrect." And what's correct in manners today may have been incorrect in the 1800's.

So there is a sense of right and wrong, correct and incorrect in this category. But one thing that makes this category different from "sin" is that sin does not change. Sin is sin no matter what culture, no matter what era. Because sin is missing the mark. And the mark is not social convention. The mark is the one Standard who never changes. Perfect Love. Still, there are often consequences for doing wrong, even in the category of social convention. And there are good reasons to take this category seriously, as we'll see in a minute.

Positive Law

The second category of right vs. wrong can also be cultural. It's the realm of "positive law." (Not in the sense of positive vs. negative, but in the sense of "posit" which means "set down." Think "deposit.") These are civil laws "set down" by our governments. Driving age. Speed limits. Mandatory school attendance. Voting age. Tax laws. Property laws. All of these can change too. Different cultures may have different laws on these issues. Or the government may decide to lower the speed limits to 55 mph on all freeways (like it did in the 1970's). Lots of laws fit this category. And the government provides consequences for breaking them. So karma is at work here too.

In this category of positive law, there can be disagreement over whether the laws themselves are right. Legislators, lobbyists, and citizens have hot debates over tax rules and other kinds of laws. This category of law is stronger than social convention, but most of these laws are not the gut-level Standard of Perfect Love that doesn't change. Still, this category is important, and most of us take positive law very seriously.

Natural Moral Law

When civil or positive laws begin to deal with natural moral law, that's when they move into the third category of right vs. wrong, the most serious level. That's the Standard in everyone, the image of Perfect Love that all people know if you ask them, "Is it right for me to murder you? Is it right for me to steal from you?"

(As we said before, people can rationalize and get so twisted in their thinking that they can figure out reasons why they think it would be "right" to steal from someone else, or even murder someone else. But usually these same people don't think you should steal from *them* or murder *them*. It's when they think of *themselves* as the victim that they know it's wrong.)

Anyway, think about Perfect Love. Does it desire life or death? The Standard is the image of God. And God *lives*. He is the *Be*ing. Existing. Life. Moses told God, "The people will want to know who sent me. What should I tell them?" God said, "Tell them I AM who I AM. Tell the people I AM sent you."[1] God is. He exists. He lives. He is *for* life. So moving toward the Standard means moving toward what brings life. And moving away from the Standard means moving toward what brings death.

Some wrongs are more unnatural than others and have a more devastating effect on us. (Although the wound heals, the scar is still there.) But every category of right and wrong should be taken seriously. Even with social convention (keep your room clean; chew with your mouth closed; cover your mouth when you cough), these rules are meant to make *life* better for everyone. Besides, while issues of social convention may not be a matter of sinning or not sinning, they *are* a matter of respecting others and obeying authorities (as long as authorities are not telling us to do gut-level wrong). Kindness and respect for others, including authority, *is* part of Perfect Love. And frankly, kindness and respect for others is just plain wisdom. That's where God operates: Wisdom.

The Way Life Works Best

A wise man learns from his mistakes. A wiser man learns from someone else's mistakes.

The bottom line is: "Right" is the way life works best. It enhances life. Fills it full. Makes it user-friendly and worth living. It's good karma at work. "Wrong" is NOT the way life works best. It diminishes life. Brings trouble. Makes life stressful and discouraging, if not hopeless. It's bad karma at work. But don't take my word for it. Do a head-gut check. Let's say. . . on the subject of cheating:

If cheating is right, then everyone should do it. Right?

What does your gut tell you?

So — good news — you can cheat on your next geometry test. Your friend sitting next to you can cheat too. Hey! Nobody has to study anymore! If cheating is right, we're *supposed* to do it. It's the way to live.

That means it's okay for your teacher to cheat you out of a good grade. And he can cheat you by giving you a test on advanced trig instead of basic geometry. Right?

So the whole class cheats — because that's the way life works best — and the teacher cheats. And after class, everyone crowds into the hall talking about how wonderful the teacher is to cheat so much and give a test on something he's never taught you. Cheating is an excellent way to live.

And your boyfriend or girlfriend is cheating on you by

dating someone else behind your back. You find out, and you celebrate. Wonderful! Cheating leads to LIFE!

Or how about mockery. If it's right, then we should be encouraging everyone to mock each other as often as possible, because it's the way to live.

While we're at it, let's throw in hypocrisy, a form of lying. So let's include lying.

What does your gut tell you?

If cheating, lying, mockery, and hypocrisy are right, we should go around saying, "Lie to me. Cheat me. Make fun of me! These help me truly live a wonderful, satisfying life!" In reality, when people treat us these ways, we complain about it. Even people who don't believe in God complain about being cheated and deceived.

"Sin is not hurtful because it is forbidden, but it is forbidden because it is hurtful."
— Benjamin Franklin[3]

That's why Jesus said, "Do to others what you would have them do to you."[2] This "Golden Rule" is a test of what's right and wrong. It puts us back in touch with our gut-level knowledge. It tells us that we have within us the Standard by which we know natural moral law (or karma).

Sin? What Sin? I Don't See Any Sin.

Sin is active and alive and life-controlling. Sin is a betrayal of yourself, of others, and of God. Betrayal is
turning your back on someone,
leaving them,
running out on them,
lying to them,
rejecting them.
So when we sin, we are lying and turning our back on others,

God, and even ourselves. Someone once said that sin takes us farther than we meant to go, we stay longer than we meant to stay, and it costs us more than we meant to pay. It's like a pebble thrown into a pond. It creates ripples that travel far beyond where the pebble plopped in.

But have you noticed that it's mostly only preachers and pastors who talk about sin? Our global, pluralistic culture shares the Buddhist viewpoint: Instead of saying a particular behavior is "sin," they say it's "inappropriate" or "unworthy." This makes people feel better and keeps everyone from feeling guilty. The truth is, as long as people don't accept God as being personal, calling sin "inappropriate behavior" is the only way to neutralize the feeling of being condemned.

> *"(Sin is) cosmic treason."*
> — *R. C. Sproul*[4]

A non-personal God can be whatever you want him to be. You can even have more than one. Just as many of us like to find Build-Your-Own Omelet or Build-Your-Own-Pizza on a menu, many of us like the concept of Build-Your-Own-God. But if God is not personal, that automatically means God is not love. Because love is personal. So the Standard is gone. If the Standard is gone, we can't miss the mark, because there's no mark to aim at. True, like all Eastern philosophies, New Age and pluralism say, "Do good, do good, do good." This sounds like a right goal. But in New Age and pluralism, each person decides for himself or herself what's good and what's not. So the placement of the mark is up to each person's opinion.

One popular opinion is that all actions are morally equal. So there's no system of good vs. evil. People who buy this philosophy feel they are breaking free from the bondage of evaluating their actions as good or bad. Their goal is to eventually realize that they never did wrong to begin with. If we say there's no such thing as natural moral law, or no such thing as a

Standard, then there's no such thing as sin. Some people try to comfort themselves by rationalizing that way.

"One reason that sin flourishes is that it is treated like a cream puff and not a rattlesnake."
— Billy Sunday, baseball player and preacher[5]

Another popular New Age opinion is that people should make contact with the Supreme Energy Source, the Divine "It" that makes up all things. This energy source and people's hearts are a seamless, wireless network that is turned on 24/7.

Christians, of course, believe this too. But Christians know that a personal God is the Supreme Energy Source in constant contact with us. Unless we break that contact. How do we break the contact? By sin.

> Jesus said, "I tell you most solemnly that anyone who chooses a life of sin is trapped in a dead-end life and is, in fact, a slave. A slave is a transient, who can't come and go at will. The Son, though, has an established position, the run of the house. So if the Son sets you free, you are free through and through." (John 8:34-36, _The Message_)

The Power

If humans could achieve goodness on their own, we would have done it by now. After all, Buddhism and Hinduism have been teaching "do good, do good, do good" since long before Jesus was born. And the laws of right living that God gave Moses have been taught since ancient times. All this teaching about the right way to live has given humans plenty of time to do good and to get better and better. Instead, we still find ourselves cheating and lying, destroying and lusting, warring and abusing. We've proved that humans are poor governors and judges for this world. But then, that's the result of sin. Sin is strong. Sin is real. Sin is alive in human hearts. And sin has the power to separate us from Perfect Love, to separate us from God. Because our own God-given power of choice energizes sin.

Sin also has power because of our worth. If we had no worth, God could just say, "Never mind; forget it."

Do a head-gut thing here:

- God didn't just "forget it," so we must be worth something to God. Right?

- Sin's power separates us from God. So if God didn't just "forget it," He must not want to be separated from us. Right?

- God is life. Separation from God is death. So sin holds the power of death, because it has the power to separate us from God.

- But is the power of sin stronger than the power of God? What does your gut tell you?

> I know how bad I've been;
> my sins are staring me down.
> You're the One I've violated, and you've seen
> it all, seen the full extent of my evil.
> You have all the facts before you;
> whatever you decide about me is fair.
> I've been out of step with you for a long time,
> in the wrong since before I was born.
> What you're after is truth from the inside out.
> Enter me, then; conceive a new true life.
> [. . .] Bring me back from gray exile,
> put a fresh wind in my sails!
> — Psalm 51:3-6, 12, The Message

Sin is not a problem for God.

From the beginning, He knew sin would exist. He knew we would miss the mark. But what concerns Him most is that we come closer to Him. Remember when we looked at pluralism earlier and saw that calling God "impersonal" lets us choose any standard we want, and then we can neutralize sin or say it doesn't exist. But that doesn't actually neutralize sin at all. It simply whitewashes sin, ignores it, sweeps it under the bed.

> "There is no saint without a past — no sinner without a future."
> Ancient Persian Mass[6]

A young man recently started to buy his first house. It looked like the perfect starter home. But before he actually bought it, he had an inspector look at it. The inspector discovered that the foundation of the house wasn't supported properly. So the house was sinking under its own weight. The floor was already slightly uneven. But the untrained eye couldn't tell. If the inspector hadn't pointed the trouble out, the young man wouldn't have known. At least not yet. But eventually the walls would have developed cracks. The floor would have tilted. The whole house would have had major problems.

That's the way it is when we try to ignore sin, or say it doesn't exist. We won't notice for awhile. But eventually we'll have major problems and begin to sink under the weight of our own sin. Sin always leads to death, spiritually, mentally, emotionally, or physically. That's karma. Ignoring the cause (sin) will not neutralize the effect (consequence).

But there *is* a way not just to neutralize sin, but to erase it altogether. It can't be done by trying to ignore our bad karma and its bad consequences. It can only be done by realizing that the condemnation for our own bad karma has been experienced already. By God incarnate as Jesus Christ. Because *we* can't get rid of sin. Only God can neutralize and erase sin.

Okay, so if God erases sin, then — three cheers — we can sin all we *want*, right? Because our sin has been erased. But do we really *want*? If that's what we really want (to choose sin), then why do we want Perfect Love? That's like saying, "I want the Standard, but I also want what's-not-the-Standard." How could we really want both?

Earlier I asked if the power of sin is stronger than the power of God. That's the same as asking if the power of death is stronger than the power of life. We know that answer, gut-level. Anyway, God answered both questions when He raised Jesus from death. The power of God paid the consequences for sin and forgave us. The power of life destroyed the power of death and opened the way for us to live forever.

> *"There is not enough darkness in all the world to put out one small candle."*
> — Anonymous[7]

God's love through Jesus means that
>   God knows our sin,
>   but takes away sin's power,
>   by receiving sin's consequence of death Himself,
>   cleansing us of sin
>   so He can perfect in us the Love
>   that's higher than our highest thoughts.

Chapter 12

Getting to the Root of Things

We like fast stuff. Fast food. Fast cash at the automated teller. High-speed internet. Instant messaging. Even instant seed-planting for gardeners. If you're into yards and gardens, maybe you've done instant planting yourself. Wherever you want a garden, you roll out a biodegradable "tape" strip that has seeds imbedded in it. Then you water it and — ta-da! — instant garden. Ready, set, grow.

The important thing about this way of planting is that the roots of the sprouting seeds grow down through the decomposing strip. You can do a similar thing with pots made out of peat or newspaper. Just plant the whole pot. The pot decomposes into the ground around it, and the roots go deep into the soil. It doesn't take a genius to see that if you planted seeds in a *plastic* pot, the roots would grow only inside the plastic and would never go very deep.

So what's the point here? Well, we all have spiritual roots, the support or foundation for our beliefs. The apostle Paul wrote that he prayed for people to be rooted in a love more excellent than knowledge: the Love of Jesus Christ. He said that then people would realize how broad and long and high and deep God's Love is, and they'd be filled up with the fullness of God.[1] Paul is definitely talking about the spiritual dimension here.

Going to the Roots

Up to this point, we've let the head-gut thing guide our way to and through the spiritual dimension. We haven't looked much at what the Bible says except to show how Jesus told us we'd discover Truth by going to our gut-level, letting God's Spirit confirm Truth to our spirits. The reason we haven't used the Bible much is because, as we discussed earlier, Truth goes deeper and is older than the Bible. Remember? It's not Truth simply because it's in the Bible; it's in the Bible because it's Truth. Paul didn't pray that the people would be filled up with the fullness of scriptures. He prayed that they would be filled with the fullness of God Himself.

> But if we keep shoving the Bible in people's faces, they often can't see past it to the Truth they know they know.

If we use the Bible like the seed tape or the peat pot to help our roots go deeper, then we get to the Source of our spiritual nourishment. Our roots grow into the "soil" of Perfect Love and begin stretching out into the width, length, height, and depth of God. But if we treat the Bible like the plastic pot, as if it were all we needed, we become root-bound and stay shallow, not finding the nourishment and freedom that's available at the Source. Jesus actually talked about this same issue. He said, "You study the scriptures because you think you have eternal life in them. But the scriptures are meant to lead you to me."[2]

It's not that the Bible isn't important. It *is* important. But if we keep shoving the Bible in people's faces, they often can't see past it to the Truth they know they know.

"The Bible says this-or-that" means nothing to someone who doesn't believe in the Bible. Or to someone who has never heard of the Bible. Or to someone who thinks the Bible is just the Christian's rule book. Or to someone who's been condemned by a person quoting the Bible. And there are a *lot* of people in those four categories. If they come to know gut-level Truth first, then the Bible will begin to make sense to them. (It's the same for you.)

Besides, I really don't think the Bible is the reason you believe. Do a head-gut check for yourself:

• Do you believe in Jesus because the Bible tells about Him?

• How do you know that the Bible is telling Truth?

• Were you there in the beginning when God created the world?

• Do you know anyone who was?

We don't have to get bent out of shape by people who believe in evolution. Why would we want to fight people who believe this theory? Fighting them is a complete waste of time, and it takes us away from the main point: There is a Being greater than humans who is at least equal to, if not greater than, the highest concept humans can conceive, which is Perfect Love. Check your gut. Is this True or not? So does your belief depend on whether the world was created in seven 24-hour days or not? I don't think so. I think you believe for a reason deeper than that. (Besides, scientists are beginning to challenge themselves on evolution.) Jesus didn't say, "They'll know you are my followers because of your stand on evolution." Or because of any other stand. He said, "They'll know you are my followers by your love."[3]

111

So do you believe because of what the Bible says? You may believe because the Bible led you to what you knew in your gut was Truth. But in that case, the Bible was simply the tool that took you there. I think if your belief is founded on the Bible, then you are in a shaky place. The only foundation you can't be shaken off of is God Himself. Perfect Love.

A Rule Book?

"Then if the Bible is not the foundation of our belief, what's the Bible for?" It's to grow us up in our relationship with God. To help us mature.

"How? By giving us rules to follow?"

Jen trudged into the den to join her Bible study group. She sighed as she sat down. "I wish God had just given us a list of rules instead of putting them in all these different books of the Bible where you have to go find them. Maybe we could just make a list of them so I could hang them up on my wall and check them off."

You actually could go through the Bible and make a rule book. In fact, some Sunday School lessons and devotional guides come awfully close to giving us a checklist on how to live. Not that it's bad to know the best way to live, but as we've seen, God takes care of this by putting His natural moral law within us. If we try to live by a checklist, it's hard not to think of God as a frowning principal keeping a report card on us. "Works well with others." "Needs improvement." "Passing." "Failing." "A, B, C, D, F."

Of course we feel more secure knowing where we stand with God. So to see a chart and know exactly how we're doing might seem like a fine way to help us feel like we're on the right track.

But wait!

If you had a check list, would you ever get all check marks or A's? Or would there always be areas in which you'd need improvement? Are there some places where you'd fail? What does your gut tell you? We can be secure knowing where we stand with God ONLY by telling Him we can't live up to His Standard of Perfect Love, and then by receiving His life and death for us. His perfect karma. Perfect Love, incarnated as Jesus Christ.

When we read about the life of Jesus, we see Perfect Love in action. We discover what perfect love is like — and Who Perfect Love is. We see Who to pattern our lives after. This Standard of Perfect Love is higher and deeper than all the rules in the world. Think of the Ten Commandments:

- "Have no other gods."

If we are pursuing Perfect Love (God), and if He is our Source and our Standard, why would we have any other gods?

- "Honor your father and mother."

If we are trying to love perfectly, why would we dishonor *any* authority?

- "Do not murder. . . commit adultery. . . steal . . . lie. . . covet."

If we are trying to pattern ourselves after Perfect Love, would we do any of these things?

If we are pursuing Perfect Love, we wouldn't even have to *know* about the Ten Commandments. We would not violate natural moral law except in a moment of human weakness, like David did when he committed adultery with Bathsheba. Even then, like David, we would *repent*, not only being sorry, but also resolving to change.

Life just isn't intended to be as rigid as much of Christian society has made it seem. We don't have to check off *any* rules. We simply keep our feet aimed in God's direction, and do our best to mirror Perfect Love in any and all situations. That far surpasses all the rules you could ever think of. But. . . if you are reading this and you just *have* to have "Christian" rules, there's only one: Love. And that's the Standard whether you can read a Bible or not.

The Story

See, there's another problem: Some people in the world still can't read. And some people, even if they can read, don't have a Bible, and don't have a way to get one. And *lots* of people who can read and do have a Bible *don't* read it, because they don't understand it. It *is* a complex book. (It's also X-rated, and if you've never read it all the way through, you might want to read a simple translation like the Message or the New Living Translation.)

Anyway, we don't need a Bible to come to believe in Jesus. But once we believe, a Bible helps grow us up in our belief. But if not by rules, then how? By *story*. Story that connects to you, gut-level. That's what the Bible is: a story of Truth. In those ancient documents, people recorded how God related to them in those days, and how they related to God. When you read what they wrote, you realize you're not so much different gut-level than they were. And God's Spirit will connect with your spirit to confirm the Truth you read.

Truth from your mouth means more to me
than striking it rich in a gold mine.
With your very own hands you formed me;
now breathe your wisdom over me so I can understand you.
— Psalm 119:72, 73, <u>The Message</u>

Most of us grew up hearing Bible stories told to us as if they were a collection like Aesop's fables (Jesus healed ten lepers; only one came back to thank Him; the moral of the story is "be thankful"). But the Bible is not a *collection* of stories; it *is* a story. If you read it as a story, you'll hear and feel, gut-level, the love of God for humans. You'll be drawn into the nearness of God's heart.

The Bible really is a pretty amazing book. God inspired its writers and recorded, through them, His incarnation in Jesus Christ. The first believers, (sometimes called the early church) agreed that those particular writings represented what Jesus' life and teachings really meant. Having these stories and teachings written down prevented them from being changed by Greek and Eastern philosophers. So the Bible keeps the story and its message pure.

When you read the Bible, the part to pay the most attention to is Jesus' life and teachings. Jesus was a storyteller, and His language was as rich as a poet's. He's the one who takes you back to gut-level, away from thinking life is just about rules. He leads you toward understanding that life is found in what Perfect Love has accomplished for you. And when you read what He says and does, gut-level, you'll be saying, "Yes. Yes. Yes!" Because Truth is written all over Jesus. He shows us God.

And then Paul's letters are like a fine steak. You have to cut into them and chew. But wow! What meat! Paul understood karma. So every time you read the word "law" in his letters, you can substitute the word "karma," and you'll see how the cause and effect of human action works.

But the most beautiful thing about the Bible is that you could read it day after day for the rest of your life, and each day you'd find a new thought, a new inspiration, something that seems like it was written just to you. That's God's Spirit connecting to the individual unique person who is *you*, and gut-level showing you that He's communicating with you through the ancient writings of those who were seeking Him just like you are. So does it diminish the importance of the Bible to say that our belief is based on the Truth that lies behind and beyond the Book? No. It makes the Bible more of a treasure, more precious. Because it's the only ancient document we have in which people recorded their actual in-the-moment experiences with our Maker.

I love your clear-cut revelation.
You're my place of quiet retreat;
I wait for your Word to renew me.
— Psalm 119:113, 114, The Message

Just remember: the Bible is not God. It is not equal to God. But it can tell you a lot about God. The Bible contains Truth. It teaches Truth. But it is not Truth Himself. As a poet once wrote, it is a lamp to our feet and a light to our path.[4] But God incarnate in Jesus Christ is the Truth, the True Light that enlightens every person in the world.[5]

> Jesus, I know Who You are,
> and I will not let go of You.

Chapter 13

So What's This Life For?

As I write this, I'm flying at 29,000 feet, hundreds of miles an hour. Our jet is weaving its way around thunderstorms, so it's a bit bumpy. It occurs to me that life is that way. We move fast, trying to stay emotionally high, weaving our way around the storms that pop up all around us. It's bumpy. And occasionally we find ourselves flying right into the storm, hanging on for our lives. I'm sure that you, like I do, sometimes wonder why. Why did God make us? Why does He want us? How can He stand us? Why does He keep this world turning?

I don't know anyone who knows the answers to those questions, although I've heard some guesses that sound pretty good. Like: God is love, and love has to have someone to give itself to. Or God wants a big family to love. You may think of more reasons.

> *The Puzzle*
> *I said, "God, I have only a small piece of the puzzle.*
> *It's not even a border side piece or a corner piece.*
> *It's one of those unidentifiable pieces*
> *that's out there in the middle somewhere*
> *and looks like so many other pieces.*
> *I have this one piece,*
> *and I don't even know where to put it."*
> *And God said, "Put it in my hand."*

Knowing exactly what happened before we came along doesn't really matter. Neither does knowing exactly what will happen after earth-life. What matters is that right now we are here on earth. We are alive. So what's the deal? What are we supposed to do?

Life on this earth is preparing us for Something. We don't know exactly what it is, but it's Something Big. Something Cosmically Important. Life on earth is our schoolroom. So what are humans supposed to learn in this global schoolroom?

1. We are not God.
2. We can never be Perfect. We miss the mark.
   (Because we are the creation, not the Creator.)
3. We need God and His Love.

That's pretty much it. The 1-2-3 of life. The easy part is looking at the 1-2-3 and saying, "Yeah, I got it." That's head-level. A good start. We can even check the gut-level and say, "Yeah, I know that I know that this is the goal." But the deal is: once it checks out at the head-gut levels, you've still only put on your dancing shoes. Now it's time to get out on the dance floor.

> ### Be Helpless
> Be helpless before Me,
> for I am your Helper.
> Be lifeless before Me,
> for I am your Life.
> Be empty before Me,
> for I am your Fullness.
> Be still before me,
> for I am your God.

Long ago Isaiah, one of *hoi christou Theou* (the "anointed of God" or "the christ of God"), wrote something that he heard God say: ". . .my word that goes out from my mouth. . .will not return to me empty, but will accomplish what I desire and achieve the purpose for which I sent it."[1] Now Jesus is the Word, the Logos. And when you accept Him as the Christ, He becomes the Image in you, and the rest of life is your growth to reflect His Image, growth toward Him as the Standard. In that sense, you are a "word" of God. And you will not return to God empty, but will accomplish what He desires and achieve the purpose for which He sent you.

Now is when we want to say, "So what is His purpose? What does He want me to DO?" Ouch! Back to karma. Stay away from DO until you get the first part down: BE. You were created as a BEing, not a DOing. Look again at the 1-2-3 of life. To know these three things, you don't have to DO anything but a head-gut check. In other words, you first need to just BE. Out of BEing, grows DOing.

Jesus knew that. When someone asked, "What's the most important rule?" Jesus answered, "Love the Lord your God with all your heart and with all your soul and with all your mind. The second most important rule is: Love your neighbor as yourself. All the Law and all the prophets are linked to these two rules."[2]

Why are the law and prophets linked to loving the Lord and loving your neighbor? Because the law is "do good, do good, do good" and the prophets wrote tirades about how the people weren't doing good and what would happen as a consequence. So Perfect Love solves the demands of both the law and the prophets.

Let's take a look at these two rules.

1. Love God with all your heart, soul, and mind. This is a BEing rule. This is gut-level who you are. You only have to breathe and have a pulse to do this.

2. AFTER you are BEing in love with God, then you are ready to DO. In fact you can't help but DO. And the DOing reflects God's Image in you: Perfect Love. Now all you have to DO is love others like you love yourself. It's the simplest rule in the world to remember, and it covers every circumstance in your life. (Of course, it's simple to remember, but just a wee bit harder to do. That's why Jesus lived perfect karma for us and died to take the consequence of our bad karma. Now when we blow it, we can let Him pick us up and dust us off, and we can try again without being damned. We also have God's Spirit as our Helper.)

Now because Jesus knows these two rules, He can go anywhere, and He fits in anywhere: any social level, any race, any culture, rich or poor or middle class, male or female, educated or uneducated, right-brained or left-brained, modern or post-modern. Because He carries God's Perfect Love. He doesn't bring with Him any certain ritual or tradition or way of walking or talking or dressing. He doesn't lay any of that on anyone. He just brings Love. And Love can flow over any barrier anywhere at any time. You can too, if you are a carrier of Love.

"Are you tired? Worn out? Burned out on religion? Come to me. Get away with me and you'll recover your life. I'll show you how to take a real rest. Walk with me and work with me — watch how I do it. Learn the unforced rhythms of grace. I won't lay anything heavy or ill-fitting on you. Keep company with me and you'll learn to live freely and lightly." — Jesus

— Matthew 11:28-30, *The Message*

The other thing to remember is that rule #1 comes before rule #2. If you get it the other way around, you've got it out of order. And getting it out of order makes it a lot harder to do. In fact, getting it out of order puts you back under karma, DOing to try to get God's favor in hopes that you can BE acceptable to Him. That's karma loud and clear. It won't work. As good as you are, you won't be able to pull it off. And if you try, you'll end up thinking that what you DO is your identity, when it's who you ARE (the BE verb) that's your identity.

> *Hunger for Me*
> *Hunger for Me as you hunger for food.*
> *Thirst for Me as you thirst for drink.*
> *I am your fullness, everything you could hope for.*
> *Find your fulfillment in Me.*

"Put God first," said Jesus, "and He'll make sure you have what you need."[3] That includes what you need to DO. So no worries, mate. BE God's. Then God will show you what to DO. In fact, He's already showing you simply by who you are and where you are.

Before God sent Moses back to Egypt to lead the people out, God asked him, "What's there in your hand?"[4] Moses held a totally ordinary shepherd's staff used for a totally ordinary job. But it was the exact thing God used to prepare Moses for a position of influence and authority. You have a schedule: studies, relationships, maybe a job or sports. As totally ordinary as your daily life might seem to you, DOing those things faithfully, as excellently as you can, prepares you for the next thing God's going to bring your way. He says, "Whoever can be trusted with very little can also be trusted with much."[5]

Now this next concept is so important that your whole relationship with God is centered around it. In fact, the whole Bible is centered around it. So we're going to camp here for a page or two. The concept is "Pro-Glo." God is the Pro. You are the Glo. It was that way in the beginning, it's that way now, and it will be that way long after this life is over.

> "Search your heart and see. . . . The way to do is to be."
> — Lao Tze [6]

So what is this Pro-Glo concept? (I know. It sounds like a floor wax. But it's an easy way to remember the concept. Besides, it makes me feel British. You know. Fab. De*lish*.) Pro-Glo is short for Provide and Glorify. Here's how it worked/works/will work forever. In the beginning, God, being God, provided everything His creation needed. Adam and Eve in the Garden simply *received* and *enjoyed* what God gave them. The whole spiritual world of angels (and any other beings who were around to watch) saw something in this. They saw who God was. They saw His Perfect Love. They saw His power. They saw His joy, peace, patience, kindness, goodness, gentleness, faithfulness, and self-control. Seeing who God is, is called *glory*.

When an Olympic athlete wins, he or she gets *glory* for awhile. For the sake of easy grammar, let's say it's "she." She has won a gold medal for gymnastics. She stands on the top tier of the stage, wearing a gold medal around her neck. Her country's flag hangs behind her. Her national anthem is played. All the cameras are focused on her. Millions of people are watching. The tv coverage shows a clip of her life in-training and at home with her family. She gets interviewed. Her picture is on the covers of magazines. There are news articles about her. Her face is on a gazillion boxes of Wheaties. Glory. Showing *who she is*. So when we *glorify* God or *bring Him glory*, we are showing who He is.

Okay. Back to the Garden. When the spiritual beings saw God's glory (who He was), they saw it in contrast to the evil they knew existed (hatred, anger, stress, impatience, ugliness, harshness, faithlessness, and loss of self-control). Next to this Darkness, God's Light was brilliant, awe-inspiring. Next to Evil, God's Perfect Love was obvious, clear as cloudless sky.

But Adam and Eve didn't know evil. Only good. Yet they were supposed to be beings with free wills, creatures of choice. Plus, other people would be coming onto the scene, because Adam and Eve were going to "multiply and fill the earth."

"When the well's dry, we know the worth of water."
—Benjamin Franklin[7]

And God would be providing, but humans would never see how great His provision and love were if they didn't know just how bad things *could* be without God's provision. They would not know who God really was. They would not be able to glorify Him. So they had to come to know evil.

Of course, that's exactly what they did by exercising their freedom to choose. And look closely. What was their choice? To provide for themselves. They decided that the fruit on the tree of the knowledge of good and evil would make them as wise as God. Why would that be so tempting? *Because if they could be as wise as God, they could provide for themselves.*

What's interesting is that this is exactly the consequence of their decision. God respected their choice, and sent them out into the world to provide for themselves. Then they found out how hard it was. In fact, they found out they couldn't do it. They still needed the Provider. That was exactly God's point. Only He is God. Only He can Love perfectly. Only He can provide perfectly.

Ever since then, people have tried to provide for themselves. If they are successful for awhile, who gets the glory?

They do. Just as it happens with the Olympic winner, people look for the ones who are succeeding in something (for the moment) and put them in the spotlight, show everyone who they are, give them glory. But no one is successful at providing for themselves all the time in every area of their lives. Karma kicks in here. So people hit the speed bumps or worse, the brick walls. Most of these stresses and disappointments and hardships are natural consequences of *somebody* trying to provide for themselves. But there's a positive side to these problems. They are meant to show us humans that we can't get it right. We need a Provider.

Hardship, aka stress, tension, pressure, trouble, strain, anxiety, struggle, trauma, angst. Hebrews 12:7 says, "Consider hardship as discipline." Discipline. That's training, not punishment. Jesus took your punishment, so hardships are not sent by God to punish you. Think of the word "self-discipline." That doesn't mean you punish yourself. It means you control yourself.

Have you ever gone through a stressful time when you felt that things were out of your control? You have to accept someone else's control, and ultimately God's. You can't do anything about what's going on, so you must rely on God to bring it all to a good end. And, though it may take time, God will. His Love always wins. Meanwhile, the stress can be a catalyst to draw you to the One Who is Perfect Love. It's training (discipline) for "letting go and letting God," as the saying goes.

When we allow God to provide (which means we receive, enjoy, and thank Him), who gets the glory? God does. We get into a tight spot in life, and we say, "God, I can't do this. Help!" When He helps, we don't say, "Hey! Look what I did!" We say, "God did that! What a Provider!" Then what happens? Other people see that we didn't do it on our own. God provided. Eventually, they start wanting the Provider for their lives too. God is glorified when others see how He provides for us.

Bottom line: If people provide for themselves, *they* get the glory. If they allow God to provide for them, *God* gets the glory. Besides, people's provision for themselves is not dependable. It's chancy and takes lots of hard work. On the other hand, God's provision for us is always dependable and requires us to rest in Him.

> *The diamond cannot be polished without friction, nor the man perfected without trials.*
> — Chinese proverb [8]

This is true in both dimensions, the spiritual as well as the physical. In the spiritual/moral realm, we know that no one loves as perfectly as God loves. But all through history there have been lots of *good* people in the world. There are lots of *good* people around even today. They can either rely on God for their goodness, or they can rely on themselves. When people rely on themselves to "do good, do good, do good," and they *achieve* a level of goodness that impresses others, who gets the glory? *They* do. But they often find that they've become their own standard, and they find it hard to live up even to their own standard!

But when people BE first, loving God with all their hearts, souls, and minds, and *then* they DO what He gives them to do with His provision of help, who gets the glory? God does. Even if other people refuse to see who God is through His provision, there's a whole host of spiritual beings who see.[9] God *will* get the glory.

You can see this Provide-Glorify concept all through the Bible. For example, God promised to give old Abraham a son. Then Sarah stepped in and tried to provide by herself. It brought all kinds of problems. But when God provided, He got the glory.

The 1-2-3 of life is about God showing who He is. In other words, His glory. Pro-Glo. God provides. We glorify. But there's a related concept. It, too, has to do with everything life is about. It's the Blessing-factor. B-factor for short.

The ancient scriptures tell about a conversation God had with Abraham. "I'll bless you," said God. "And you will be a blessing. That way, all the people of the earth will be blessed."[10] To *bless* someone means to cause them to prosper, to bring good things to them, to help them succeed. God set up the B-factor as His modus operandi, His method of working. God was saying, "Abraham, whatever I do for you to help you succeed, whatever I give you that makes you prosper, you are to turn around and use it to help others succeed and prosper. That way, all the people of the earth will prosper."

Remember, this was before God gave the laws to Moses. Before the Ten Commandments. There was only karma, the natural moral law that existed because of the Standard in all people. And God was not giving Abraham rules here. He was simply saying, "Love like I love you." Sound familiar? ("The most important rule is to love the Lord with all your heart and soul and mind. Then love your neighbor as yourself. All laws are linked to this." - Jesus)

Basically, God was telling Abraham to head toward Perfect Love, because God would provide for Abraham out of His Perfect Love. And He asked Abraham to mirror Him, to reflect the Image of Perfect Love to others. That would accomplish two things.

First, it would show Abraham that He needed God. A mirror can't reflect something it's not facing. So Abraham would have to keep himself turned toward God. When he succeeded, it would be because he was reflecting God. When he failed, he would have to depend on God to provide patience and mercy and help.

Second, when Abraham *did* reflect God's love by helping others prosper, then it brought glory to God. It showed who God is. People saw God's provision in Abraham's life. The God-to-human relationship became clear.

> Lord, make me an instrument of Your peace.
> Where there is hatred, let me sow love
> Where there is injury, pardon.
> Where there is doubt, faith.
> Where there is despair, hope.
> Where there is darkness, light; and
> Where there is sadness, joy.
> — Saint Francis of Assisi[11]

Pro-Glo and the B-factor. God provides, humans glorify. God blesses us, we bless others (so they can see how great God is — there's glory again). That's how God set up life for us. Everything points to the fact that He wants to be known for who He is, and He wants to be chosen for who He is. Just like we do.

That's one of the interesting things about God. He never asks anything of us that He has not already done Himself. For example, we want to be known for who we are, and we want to be chosen for who we are. God has done just that. He knows each of us at the deepest level of the spirit. Even if the whole world misunderstands you, God knows exactly who you are and how you were uniquely designed. And He has chosen you. He not only loves you. He *likes* you. He enjoys you.

So open your heart to God and say, "Welcome. You can live here. Remodel if you need to. Redecorate if you want. My heart is yours as long as you want it." Then God will smile and say, "As long as I want? How about forever? *My* pleasure." That's *your* glory, God seeing you for who you really are and who you were really made to be: a son or daughter of Divine Royalty. The King's child.

So within us is God's Image,
which shows us Truth,
which is the Standard,
which is Perfect Love,
which is *the* Christ in us (named Jesus),
Who is *our* hope of glory.[12]

Where we are so far:

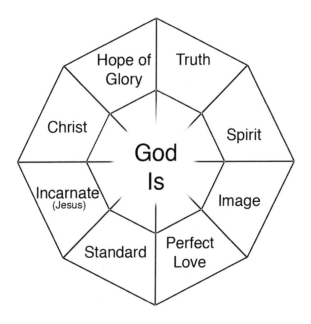

Chapter 14

Dancing
with the
Divine

In the last chapter, I said that doing the head-gut check helps us find the Truth we know we know, but that head-knowledge and gut-knowledge are simply the equivalent to putting on your dancing shoes. We took a good look at the 1-2-3 of life on the dance floor and saw our goal: Pro-Glo and the B-factor. Let's get down to specifics now and learn a few dance steps. One caveat: I can only point you in the right direction. Your partner, God, will lead in the dance, and He'll end up showing you steps I don't even know. But I can get you started.

<u>Dance With Me</u>
You said, "Dance with Me —
Take off your shoes and dance.
Let us fly among the stars
and sail past the moon,
Spirits soaring, wild and free.
I'm the Wind of heaven — lightest breath
rejoicing, lilting, carefree —
But deep and awesome, other-sided,
roaring gale, lashing at evil,
sweeping away the defiant and proud."
With bated breath I look away
from the greatness

I know is there,
            and dare not gaze on You
            for fear of melting.
My physics cannot endure You —
            Your deep brilliance,
            Your overwhelming wisdom,
            Your pulsing power.
If it were not for Your lavish love,
            I'd never even hope
            to see or hear a piece
                  of You.
But You whisper.
            You hum.
            You gently come.
And Your fingertips to mine
            speak Your grace,
Your favor extended,
            humble love of King and Counselor,
            looking for love returned.
Not duty,
            not performance,
            but love.
Love to love,
            hand to hand,
            heart to heart,
            spirit to Spirit,
We will dance, fly among the stars,
            sail past the moon,
Spirits soaring wild and free.

1. Prayer

I spent at least a whole year in college wondering why I had to pray. After all, God already knows what we need before we ask. What could I say that He didn't already know? Later, I realized I had totally missed the point. Prayer is the most awesome thing we do. It's your spirit soaking, bathing, swimming in the Spirit of God. It's part of the Divine Dance, spirit to Spirit. A poet I know was talking about reading poetry every day without feeling like you had to analyze it. He said, ". . . just like some people pray every day, *not to entreat God, but just to be with Him.*" I thought, yes. That's why we pray. Just to be with Him.

Listen to how some other people describe prayer.[1]

"Real prayer comes not from gritting our teeth but from falling in love."

(Richard Foster, writer and teacher)

"I like to think of prayer as a conversation between two friends who love and understand each other. Prayer is the key that opens the door to a whole new world."

(Hope MacDonald, author)

"Oh, this thing of keeping in constant touch with God, of making him the object of my thought and the companion of my conversations, is the most amazing thing ever ran across."

(Frank Laubach, missionary, the Philippines, 1920s to 1940s)

"Prayer is not so much a way to find God as a way of resting in him. . .who loves us, who is near to us."

(Thomas Merton, early 1900s)

"Prayer is the deepest thing we do."
(E. Stanley Jones, missionary to India)

"Prayer is not asking. Prayer is putting oneself in the
hands of God, at his disposition, and listening to his
voice in the depths of our hearts."
(Mother Theresa)

"We can read all the books that have ever been written
about prayer, but until we actually choose. . .to pray,
we will never learn."
(Hope MacDonald, author)

Prayer is just like talking to your best friend. You can do
it anytime, anywhere, and say anything. You don't have to bow
your head and close your eyes. You can do it out loud or
silently. Sometimes, you won't even use words at all. You'll just
know He's there loving you, and you are there loving Him, and
that's all that matters: you focusing on Him and He focusing on
you. That brings us to the next specific.

2. Meditation

Some people say that meditating is like a cow chewing
her cud. She swallows her lunch and then brings it back up to
chew on it again and again. Funky metaphor. But not too far
from accurate. Meditation is letting your spirit think on a quality
of God or a verse from the ancient scriptures. You chew on it
over and over again. Hence the cud metaphor. Since we're
talking gut-level, maybe that's a good way to look at it. Or
maybe chewing gum would be a more tasteful way of saying it.
Because we're trying to get as much flavor as possible out of the

scripture or thought we're meditating on.

> These are the words in my mouth;
> these are what I chew on and pray.
> Accept them when I place them
> on the morning altar,
> O God, my Altar-Rock,
> God, Priest-of-My-Altar.
> — Psalm 19:14, *The Message*

You may already have a way you like to meditate. If not, I'll give you two examples here. One you've probably done, maybe without even thinking of it as meditation. It's what God said: "Be still and know that I am God."[2] It can happen anywhere, but for lots of people it happens outdoors. (I think that's because we were created to live in a garden.) You just sit and look at the stars, or the tops of the trees, or storm clouds, or anything else in nature, and you wonder about God, about how great He is, how loving, how creative. Think of how you could describe Him: Composer, Musician, Sculptor, Painter, Author. You can, of course, do this indoors as well. This way of meditation is described by one author as "union attainable through simple awe."[3]

A second way to meditate is to read a scripture and just think about it. Think about it not only at head-level, but also at gut-level. Most of the Psalms are good for this. Some of the book of

> *"Thou hast made us for Thyself, and the heart of man is restless until it finds its rest in Thee."*
> *— Saint Augustine* [4]

Isaiah makes great food for meditation. Jesus' teachings do too, of course. And one of my favorites is Job, chapters 38-41. In Job 42:2, Job says, "I know that you (God) can do all things." Just for practice, let's meditate on that for a minute or so. It won't take long. We'll read the verse several times, but each time, we'll focus on only one word and think about what it means. (I'll bold the word.) Here goes:

"**I** know that you (God) can do all things."
Who knows: your parents? your friend? No. **I**. Gut-level.

"I **know** that you (God) can do all things."
I guess? I suspect? I doubt? I think maybe? No. I **know**.
Gut-level.

"I know that **you (God)** can do all things."
Who can do all things? Me? The government? No. **God**.
Only God.

"I know that you (God) **can do** all things."
Can try? Can wish? Might be able to do? No. **Can do**.

"I know that you (God) can do **all things**."
Some things? Many things? No. **All** things. What kinds
of things has He done, is He doing now, in your life?

If you choose to meditate this way, let God lead your
spirit to wonder, and roll these thoughts over and over. You're
not looking for answers (although you might find some). You're
resting with the questions and the mystery of God. And that
brings us to our next specific in the Dance with the Divine.

3. Worship
There are two ways to look at worship: macro and
micro.

Macro worship is the big picture. If you've given yourself to God, then your whole life is essentially worship. Because
you are dedicated to God, everything you do is dedicated to

Him. As Paul wrote, we are "living sacrifices, holy and pleasing to God — this is your spiritual act of worship."[5] So whatever we do, we work at it with all our heart as though we're working for God.[6]

In fact, one definition of worship is that it expresses the wonder and gratitude of our hearts to God. So anything we do that expresses our love, wonder, and gratitude is worship. But one of my favorite definitions actually has no words. And it came from a five-year-old girl. She said, "Worship is. . . ," and then she blew a kiss upward. Wow! Perfect!

So while the *macro* of worship is our whole life, the *micro* of worship is the particular things we do to connect with God. Have you ever heard the theory of "wormholes" in space?[7] They're supposed to be like tubes or tunnels that are shortcuts allowing travel at faster-than-light-speed between two points in the universe or from one universe or dimension to another. Well, the particular things we do to worship are like wormholes that connect us to God. Prayer and meditation connect us to God. So they're part of worship. You may have certain rituals you do at your church that are part of connecting you to God. Dance, song, drama. Anything can be worship if it expresses your love, wonder, and gratitude to God.

> "You called, you cried, you shattered my deafness, you sparkled, you blazed, you drove away my blindness, you shed your fragrance, and I drew in my breath, and I pant for you."
> — Saint Augustine [8]

4. Reading the Bible

We talked about this a couple of chapters ago. I include it in this list, because it's one of the ways to dance. Just a reminder: When you read, keep in mind that the people in the Old Testament were looking at God through the eyeglasses of law, so they viewed Him as angry and vengeful. So when you get to a Psalm that talks about violence and destruction, know that this is not God as Jesus showed Him. Jesus said that it's the enemy who comes to steal and kill and destroy. Jesus came to give us beautiful, deep, full life.[9]

> "I have read many books, but the Bible reads me."
> — Anonymous[10]

The Bible is like a mine, and reading it can be like digging for treasure. You can end up richer in spirit than you ever dreamed. One of the best ways to read it is to journal your way through.

Get yourself a notebook of some kind. On the inside of the front cover, write one or two things you want God to teach you about. Then start reading. You can do a chapter a day, or four chapters a day. (Four or five chapters a day will get you through the whole thing in about a year.) Or just start with the Psalms or the Proverbs. Or just go through the New Testament. Don't bite off more than you can chew. (Cud again. Sorry.) Anyway, as you read, look for those things you wrote on the inside cover. When you find something that deals with that subject, copy it down in your journal, along with the date and any thoughts you may have about it.

For example, let's say you want to know about *glory*. Every time you read a verse that has the word *glory* in it, you write it down. Pretty soon, you'll begin understanding more about it, so that when you get to a verse that doesn't say *glory*,

> ### Wick and Candle
> As a wick is to a candle,
> So My word is to you.
> It will be ignited within you.
> Don't forget to come to Me for lighting.
> As the flame burns, you will glow
> and spread My light far and near,
> not without some pain,
> but I will be with you.
> I will work in you My will,
> My desires.

but does talk about the concept, you'll write that down too. After going through the Bible like this, you'll know a lot about glory, and who taught you? God's Spirit. You can, of course, use any subject that you're curious about: worship, death, gratitude, friendship, whatever.

Another way to do this is not to look for any specific word or concept, but just be open each day for any verse that seems to jump out at you. After you've read a chapter, for example, go back and ask which verse seemed to "burn" into your spirit. Then write that in your journal. Of course, you may not have found a verse that day. You won't find one *every* day. But this is a way to grow closer to God.

> God's Word is better than a diamond,
> better than a diamond set between emeralds.
> — Psalm 19:10, <u>The Message</u>

5. What about church?

The church is not a building or a denomination. The church is not rituals, not a set of beliefs. People are the church. YOU are the church. You and other people who know that Jesus is the Image, the Standard, the Perfect Love, the Christ, the Way, the Truth, the Life.

You see, Love seeks community. Life seeks community. A personal God seeks community. So whether there are ten people who get together in someone's living room, or three who gather at a coffee house, or two thousand who get together in a huge building, it doesn't matter. Together, you are the church. And let's face it: We need each other. The whole world is seeking community. That's a gut-level Truth. Community is one thing God came to give us through Jesus. Because the only way community holds together successfully for any length of time is if there's Love in there somewhere. And the more people in the group who live by that Love, the more peaceful the group will be. Because the fact is, no two people can exist together in harmony. Not even the church. Unless there's Love.

> Martin Luther talks about the Bible: "First I shake the whole (apple) tree, that the ripest fruit might fall. Then I climb the tree and shake each limb, and then each branch and then each twig, and then I look under each leaf."[11]

Note: The five things listed above are <u>not rules</u>.
They're just different ways you can dance.

One Last Why

One other subject before we're done. We've talked about "why life?" Let's tackle the subject of death for a minute. I don't know where you are emotionally, but I know that sometimes it seems like it's easier to die than to live. Life is hard. (This comes as a shock to some people.) And sometimes it seems like there's too much bad stuff happening in the world, or things are too intense in your own life. We sometimes think we'd be better off checking out right now. But that's because we're gazing at our own navels. If you feel that way, look up and out. Your life has a purpose: to bring God glory. And your death will have a purpose: to bring God glory. So you will die for *His* purpose, not yours.

<u>Trouble and Ransom</u>

Trouble and ransom.
Turbulent times.
Raging waters and white rivers.
In the midst, I am God.
In the midst, I am He who overtakes the rivers.
So take the wine. Wine of laughter.
Wine of singing and song.
For the raging rivers will not overrun
My wonderful one, My beloved and esteemed,
whose heart is holy, pure, and true.
Crushed with many blows, yet rising to serve.
Beaten with many offenses, yet higher now than ever
Because of my strong right arm.
I have done this, says the Lord.
Grace and mercy are yours,
and pardon beyond belief.
Relief and strength are yours
from My own right hand.

Most of us are afraid of death. Actually, death stings only because of sin which brings separation from God. And since Jesus has taken all your sin, death has lost its sting. In fact, Jesus said, ". . . those who listen to my message and believe in God who sent me have eternal life. They will never be condemned for their sins, but they have already passed from death to life."[12] You've already started eternity. Now. So death is simply passing over from this temporary dimension into the True dimension of Reality. (Talk about a wormhole!)

But it's not yours to decide the when or how of death. Only God knows when and where and how your death will bring Him the most glory. When that time comes, He will extend His hand to you, and you'll reach out and grasp it and find that it's solid and firm and real. And you will pass over. It's that simple. And what you'll find then is beyond anything I could ever hope to describe to you. God will provide, and you will enjoy and glorify. The dance will continue, and you will fit in so perfectly, you'll say, "*This* is what I was created for."

Life with God is really what everyone is looking for. Have you ever felt a kind of sadness, a yearning in your heart for something somewhere that you just can't quite describe? It's like wanting to go home, but not having a home to go to. You want it so badly it hurts, but you can't get there. The writer George MacDonald described it as being "haunted with the scent of unseen roses."[13] That's your longing for the other dimension. If you haven't experienced it, you will someday. Meanwhile, remember: **Love trumps karma**. Always.

Life is supposed to be a dance with the Divine One. The music has been playing since before the beginning of time. I think it's your turn. Your Partner is waiting for you. Are you ready to dance?

As a child of God, you hold this treasure within you, because you were made in God's image:

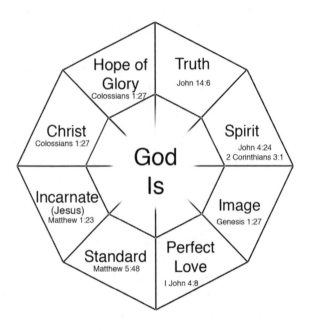

**God will full-fill all of this in you and for you,
if you'll give Him permission to dance with you.**

A down-loadable leader's study guide is available online for those who want to use this book as a 13-week course of study. You can find it at www.lovetrumpskarma.com.

End Notes

Chapter 1:

1. The five precepts of Buddhism were paraphrased by Ken Rideout from the book <u>Buddhism Explained: An Introduction to the Teachings of Lord Buddha</u> by Bhikku Khantipalo, Mahamkut Rajavidyalaya Press, Bangkok, 1989.

2. From Exodus 20 in the Bible.

Chapter 2:

1. Matthew 5:27, 28, 43-45, NLT

2. Matthew 7:28, 29

3. Matthew 5-6

4. John 7:46

5. Luke 24:32

6. John 14:6, NLT; John 15:26, NLT; Romans 8:16, NIV

Chapter 3:

1. George Sweeting, comp., <u>Great Quotes and Illustrations</u> (Waco, Texas: Word, 1985) 247.

Chapter 4:

1. Genesis 1:27, 2:7, NLT

2. Cyrus: Isaiah 44:28 - 45:6 (See also 2 Chronicles 36:21ff, and Ezra 1.)

   Balaam: Numbers 22 - 24

   Nebuchadnezzar: Daniel 2, Daniel 4 (especially verse 31)

   Cornelius: Acts 10:1-8

   The centurion: Matthew 8:5-13

   The Syro-Phoenician woman: Mark 7:24-30

   The Samaritan woman: John 4

3. Walter J. Ong, Hopkins, the Self, and God. (Toronto: U of Toronto P, 1986) 144.

Chapter 5:

1. Gerhard Kittel, ed., trans. Geoffrey W. Bromley, The Theological Dictionary of the New Testament, vol IV (Grand Rapids: Eerdmans, 1967) 84.

2. John 1:1, 4, 9, NRSV

3. T. O. Ling, A Dictionary of Buddhism: A Guide to Thought and Tradition, 97.

   Phra Khantipalo, Buddhism Explained (Bangkok: Mahamakut Rajavidyalaya, 1989) 1.

4. John B. Noss, Man's Religions, (New York: Macmillan, 1963), 209.

   Swami Nikhilananda, "The Nature of Reality," Sri Ramakrishna Centre, New York, 28 November 2000 <http://www.hinduism.co.za>.

5. John A. Hutchison, Paths of Faith (New York: McGraw, 1969) 223-229.

   Lao Tzu, Tao Te Ching, trans. James Legge (Mineola, New York: Dover, 1997).

6. Richard Martin, ed. Approaches to Islam in Religious Studies (Boston: Oneworld, 2001) 29.

Chapter 6:

1. George Sweeting, comp., <u>Great Quotes and Illustrations</u> (Waco, Texas: Word, 1985) 191.

2. Dhammapada 5 and 223 as quoted in <u>Buddhism: The Religion in Thailand</u>, 6.

3. Gerhard Kittel, ed., <u>The Theological Dictionary of the New Testament</u>, vol. IV (Grand Rapids: Eerdmans) 85.

4. Sweeting, 69.

5. Gerald F. Lieberman, <u>3,500 Good Quotes for Speakers</u> (New York: Doubleday, 1983) 217.

6. Bhikku Khantipalo,<u> Buddhism Explained: An Introduction to the Teachings of Lord Buddha</u> (Bangkok: Mahamkut Rajavidyalaya Press, 1989), 193.

Chapter 7:

1. George Sweeting, comp., <u>Great Quotes and Illustrations</u> (Waco, Texas: Word, 1985) 69.

2. Harry Verploegh, comp. <u>3000 Quotations from the Writings of George MacDonald</u>. (Grand Rapids: Revell, 1996) 314.

3. Sweeting, 168.

Chapter 8:

1. George Sweeting, comp., <u>Great Quotes and Illustrations</u> (Waco, Texas: Word, 1985) 248.

2. Sweeting, 150.

3. Sweeting, 76.

4. John 17:3

5. "Eternal Life," <u>Holman Bible Dictionary</u>, 1991.

Chapter 9:

1. Matthew 11:28, John 3:16, Matthew 5:2-12, Matthew 5:48

2. George Sweeting, comp., <u>Great Quotes and Illustrations</u> (Waco, Texas: Word, 1985), 49.

3. James N. Frey. How to Write a Damn Good Mystery. (New York: St. Martin's, 2004) 9.

4. Sweeting, 48.

5. Deborah DeFord, ed. Quotable Quotes. (Pleasantville, New York: Reader's Digest 1997) 24.

6. Alan Paton. Cry, the Beloved Country. (1948; New York: MacMillan, 1987) 39.

7. James Dalton Morrison. Masterpieces of Religious Verse. (New York: Harper, nd) 137.

Chapter 10:

1. John 3:17

2. Proverbs 16:18

3. George Sweeting, comp., Great Quotes and Illustrations (Waco, Texas: Word, 1985) 134.

4. Don Richardson. Eternity in Their Hearts, (Ventura, CA: Regal, 1981).

5. Colossians 1:15, Hebrews 1:3

6. Paraphrased from Matthew 16:16, 17

Chapter 11:

1. Exodus 3:13, 14

2. Matthew 7:12

3. Benjamin Franklin, Poor Richard's Almanack (Mount Vernon, New York: Peter Pauper, nd).

4. George Sweeting, comp., Great Quotes and Illustrations (Waco, Texas: Word, 1985) 232.

5. Sweeting, 232.

6. Deborah Deford, ed., Quotable Quotes (Pleasantville, New York: Reader's Digest, 1997) 112.

7. Sweeting, 144.

Chapter 12:
1. Ephesians 3:17-19
2. John 5:39
3. John 13:35
4. Psalm 119:105
5. John 1:9

Chapter 13:
1. Isaiah 55:10, NIV
    (A reminder: *hoi christou Theou* is the term used for prophets in Psalm 105:15)
2. Matthew 23:37, 38
3. Matthew 6:33
4. Exodus 4:2
5. Luke 16:10
6. George Sweeting, comp., Great Quotes and Illustrations (Waco, Texas: Word, 1985) 165.
7. Benjamin Franklin, Poor Richard's Almanack (Mount Vernon, New York: Peter Pauper, nd).
8. Sweeting, 97.
9. Ephesians 3:10, 11
10. Genesis 12:2
11. Sweeting, 38.
12. Colossians 1:27

Chapter 14:
1. Sources for quotes:
    Foster - Prayer: Finding the Heart's True Home, Foster, HarperCollins.
    MacDonald - Change the World School of Prayer Manual, World Literature Crusade.

Laubach and Merton - <u>Streams of Living Water</u>, Foster, HarperCollins.

Jones - <u>The Unshakable Kingdom and the Unchanging Person</u>.

Mother Theresa - As quoted in "Jonathan's Arrow," November 2000 issue.

2. Psalm 46:10

3. Peter Matthiessen, <u>The Snow Leopard</u> (New York: Penguin, 1978) 249.

4. George Sweeting, comp., <u>Great Quotes and Illustrations</u> (Waco, Texas: Word, 1985) 212.

5. Romans 12:1

6. Colossians 3:23

7. Also known as the Einstein-Rosen Bridge.

8. Sweeting, 170.

9. John 10:10

10. Sweeting, 29.

11. Sweeting, 34.

12. John 5:24

13. As quoted in <u>The Problem of Pain</u> by C.S. Lewis (1940, New York: Harper, 1996) 153.

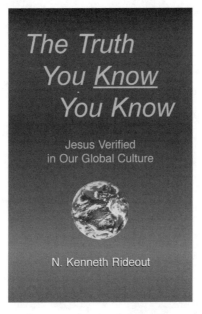